Building a Christian Marriage

Building a Christian Marriage
11 Essential Skills

Wipf & Stock
PUBLISHERS
Eugene, Oregon

KATHLEEN FINLEY

Wipf and Stock Publishers
199 W 8th Ave, Suite 3
Eugene, OR 97401

Building a Christian Marriage
11 Essential Skills
By Finley, Kathleen
ISBN: 1-59752-595-2
Copyright©2000 by Finley, Kathleen
Publication date 3/1/2006
Previously published by Loyola Press, 2000

Contents

Foreword by Mitch Finley   vii

Acknowledgments   ix

A Word to the Seeker   xi

A Good Marriage Is Countercultural   1

The Catholic Vision of Marriage   11

Skill One: Learn to Love Yourself   21

Skill Two: Let Others Get Close   35

Skill Three: Grow Up   47

Skill Four: Understand Your Family Background   61

Skill Five: Communicate Effectively   75

Skill Six: Examine Gender Roles   91

Skill Seven: Get Comfortable with Sex   101

Skill Eight: Spend Time and Money Wisely   119

Skill Nine: Grow in the Spiritual Life   131

Skill Ten: Be Open to Being a Parent   153

Skill Eleven: Get Ready to Change and Grow   165

Skills Review and Blessing Prayer   183

Appendix: Tools for
Marriage Preparation and Enrichment   194

Suggested Reading   207

Bibliography   210

Foreword

After being married to the author of this book for more than a quarter century, I can say with all honesty that the best insights I have about marriage I learned from her. Actually, when we were newlyweds, I knew far more about marriage than I do now. With our silver anniversary in the bag, marriage is a bigger mystery to me than it ever was before.

By "mystery" I do not mean "puzzle" or "conundrum" — although marriage is sometimes that as well. Rather, I use the term in its theological sense, where a mystery is a reality that transcends the human intellect but fills the human heart, where a mystery is a human experience that reveals God's love. In other words, there is no place I find God's love more evident than in our marriage.

The author of this book is not just someone who took it into her head one day to write a book about marriage.

Kathleen Finley has many years of experience as a teacher of Catholic and secular college courses on marriage and as a gifted counselor who helps couples prepare for marriage. Because she is so good at what she does, it's not unusual for engaged couples to ask her help beyond the minimum counseling in which they may be required to participate. Many people would tell you that Kathleen Finley helped them to understand, in ways they will never forget, how to have a lasting marriage. Few authors and counselors have as deep an understanding of the sacrament of marriage, and of marriage in general, as the author of this book.

In my admittedly biased but experienced opinion, you are about to read an inspired book. Whether you are looking for practical knowledge about marriage or realistic ideals to strive for in marriage, you will find what you want in these pages. Fair warning, however: when you read the last page, you will wish the book had been twice as long.

MITCH FINLEY

Acknowledgments

I offer thanks to many people who, in different ways, made this work possible. I am grateful to the engaged couples and students with whom I have worked through the years; the couples my husband and I have worked with for many years on marriage preparation weekends; and the editors at Loyola Press, especially LaVonne Neff, Jim Manney, and, last but certainly not least, Kass Dotterweich, who, as a longtime friend, was far more than an editor in helping this book come to birth.

A Word to the Seeker

Most young adults I come in contact with want to be married. They want to stay married. They want to hear a positive answer to the question, Will my marriage work?

I hear the question asked in the marriage courses I teach in two colleges in eastern Washington State. I hear it in the marriage preparation and enrichment workshops my husband and I give. I hear it year after year from the couples I work with in marriage preparation.

Some of the people who ask it are already married and are grappling with difficulties in the early years of married life. Many are not married. They want to be, but they are afraid their marriages will fail as so many do these days.

I cannot promise these people that they will succeed. The decision to marry is one of the riskiest of human choices. It's an open-ended commitment to a future together with another person. We can't control the future. It will bring set-backs and difficulties as well as joys and pleasant surprises, and we do not know how these will play out in the years ahead.

But I *can* say that your chances for a successful and ful-filling marriage are great, greater than you may think. Years of working with newly married and soon-to-be-married couples have convinced me that sensible preparation and intelligent problem solving really work. They make marital success and happiness easier to achieve.

There's another crucial factor in marital success — an awareness of the spiritual dimension of marriage. Your life with your spouse or your spouse-to-be is about more than the two of you. It's a source of grace, a gift from God. A marriage centered on God becomes a life-giving gift to many others.

So I can say with confidence that you *can* succeed in your marriage. I know many couples who have succeeded. Through my work with them and through years of work in marriage preparation and counseling, I have a good idea of the skills and attitudes needed to bring marital success within your reach.

That, in a nutshell, is what this book is about.

Some Basics

Let's begin with some assumptions that underlie the way I think about marriage. I have many convictions about marriage, most of which I will share with you in the course of this book, but these four assumptions flow through everything else I will say.

1. *Marriage is much more a process than a state of being.* It makes more sense to think about marrying your spouse than being married. In many ways a marriage license is a learner's permit to keep learning about one another. And the many elements of your married life are interconnected. Change in one area affects all the others. Sensitivity to these interconnections, as well as patience and continual attention to your marriage, yields great rewards.

2. *Marriages need support.* It's not your spouse and you against the world. Married couples need support from others in order to be strong. This support can come from other couples, from your extended family, from your church and community, from mentors and counselors. You will need to look for that support; it won't just happen.

3. *Married people need skills — today more than ever.* Married couples today face challenges that previous generations seldom had to cope with. These include the flux in gender roles, intense economic pressures, the need for extended periods of education, rapid social change, and expectations for marriage and relationships heavily influenced by a ubiquitous, secular mass media. We need a tool kit

A WORD TO THE SEEKER

of skills to cope with all this, tools our parents and grand-parents didn't need as urgently.

4. *A Christian approach to marriage can make all the difference.* In my view, the Catholic Christian way of thinking about and living out marriage embodies powerful wisdom about married life. It also makes available the best source of strength — the grace of God.

I doubt that any of these basic notions will strike you as astoundingly novel or surprising. But they are important to keep in mind as we explore the keys to a lasting marriage.

What You Will Find Here

This book will present a vision for marriage and a tool kit of skills to help you make that vision a reality.

The vision for marriage in this book is a Christian one. It is sketched out in the next two chapters. The chapter "A Good Marriage Is Countercultural" (page 1) argues a point that people already sense about marriage in modern society: marriage, in several important and fundamental ways, must be a countercultural institution if it is to be strong and flourishing. The chapter "The Catholic Vision of Marriage" (page 11) presents the countercultural vision of the Catholic tradition, which conceives of marriage as a sacramental union established by God to point the partners to God.

A WORD TO THE SEEKER

Faith contributes to a marriage in three ways: it gives the husband and wife *vision* about who they are and what they are called to become, *energy* for the daily living of their commitment of marriage, and *strength* for the tough times.

The remaining chapters are about the skills needed to build a healthy, satisfying marriage relationship. I've selected eleven areas. These areas and the skills related to them are presented in the next eleven chapters of the book, one area per chapter. They are self-esteem, intimacy, personal maturity, family systems, communication, gender roles, sexuality, money and work, spirituality, parenthood, and fidelity.

Again, most married people — and single people who seriously contemplate marriage — are aware of the importance of all these issues and questions. You've probably thought about them all and even grappled with them. However, I believe that both partners in marriage need a basic proficiency in all of these areas in order to have a lasting marriage. The goal of this book is to guide you toward achieving this basic competence.

Each chapter ends with questions for reflection that will help you apply and understand the topic of that chapter. The final chapter is a cumulative skills review. You can return to this chapter periodically to note your progress and target those areas where further work is needed. At the end of the final chapter, I offer a blessing prayer for all those considering the sacred vocation of marriage. The appendix includes a listing of resources for both marriage preparation and marriage enrichment. I have also provided suggestions for further reading and a bibliography.

How to Use This Book

This book is about getting marriage off to a good start. It is written primarily for single people preparing for marriage and for those who might consider themselves newlyweds — couples in the early stages of their marriage. It has grown out of years of work in the classroom and in Catholic marriage ministry with men and women, most of whom are between twenty and thirty-five years old. Most were single when I first met them. Virtually all of them now are married — and I fervently hope they are still improving the skills they began to learn when they were single.

If you are married, engaged, or committed to a serious relationship with someone, I invite you to go through this book with your partner. Discuss the material. Pay special attention to the reflection questions at the end of each chapter. Your different reactions to the issues raised in these pages will tell you a lot about each other. There will be differences, I assure you. Do not be frightened by them. You really wouldn't want to have it otherwise. You are different people building a common life together. Your differences are a source of great strength — as well as areas of actual or potential conflict.

If you are single, read the book on your own and examine your skill levels. I think you will find that your thinking about marriage will be enriched and that your skills for marriage and other relationships will be fortified.

This book can also be for people who have been married for a while. After all, marriage is a process. We can always improve in the ways we love our spouses. You will find useful ideas in these pages about crucial marriage skills.

Finally, this book can be used by groups. It is easily adaptable for use in Catholic marriage preparation courses and in high school and college classes.

Marriage — especially today — is an exciting adventure, a delight, and a comfort for each of the spouses as well as a source of inspiration for those around them. My husband and I have learned from many sources in the course of our twenty-five years of marriage. I hope this book can be one of those life-giving sources of help for you.

A Good Marriage Is Countercultural

Jason and Marie were friends for several years before their relationship became serious and romantic. Now, as they look at the prospect of marriage, they are concerned by what they see. There are divorces and remarriages in both of their extended families, and they know of two couples who are still together but seem deeply unhappy. Jason and Marie wonder if marriage is really a good life choice for them and, if they do marry, how they can make their marriage better than most.

Consider the questions Jason and Marie are asking. They're not asking, "Is this person the one I should marry?" Rather they're saying something sad and a little frightening: "Should I ever be married at all, to anyone? Does any marriage have a chance?"

Single people have customarily taken the great step of marriage with solemnity and, sometimes, dread. But today a whole generation seems to contemplate marriage with fear. It's hard enough to find that special person to fall in love with and marry. How awful to suspect that your marriage would fail even if you found the right person.

Marriages are under tremendous pressure today. The marriages that Jason and Marie observe among their family members and friends are not exceptions. There are more divorces than ever. Many married people seem to be unhappy, ground down by discouragement and problems. Commitment and faith — the foundations of marriage — seem scarcer than ever.

When we look realistically at the context for marriage today, we find not only fewer social supports for a lasting marriage but also higher expectations of what marriage should be. Compared to past generations, we want more from marriage today, but we give it less support.

Why is this? Let's take a look at the society within which we live our marriages — particularly its values.

Marriage under Siege

In important ways, many of our culture's values are at war with families — and with marriages. Here are some of those values:

The desire for more. We live in the "United States of Advertising," to use the apt phrase of psychologist Mary Pipher.

We are barraged by messages telling us that we don't have enough and that we need to work harder and buy more if we are to be happy. A word has been coined for this overconsumption that is forced upon us: *affluenza*. People stricken with affluenza pursue material possessions at the expense of their relationships.

But you don't need a bad case of affluenza to feel the pressure. Consider the ever increasing number of families in which both parents work outside the home — and often earn less than in the past — to meet basic needs as well as to respond to the demands for more. They have only the leftovers of time and energy for spouse and family, and children are placed in someone else's care. As Pipher puts it, "If families just let the culture happen to them, they end up fat, addicted, broke, with a house full of junk and no time."

The tendency to do rather than to be. Marriages and families are not programs and projects. You don't build a healthy marriage simply by doing things. Rather, a marriage is a place where we can be ourselves — a refuge from the world of doing. Yet we are barraged by activities. Everyone, even toddlers, has full daily schedules. As the patient tells the doctor in a recent cartoon, "I'm learning how to relax, Doctor, but I want to relax *better* and *faster! I want to be on the cutting edge of relaxation!*"

A student of mine from Indonesia made some shrewd observations about the impact of busyness on married couples:

A GOOD MARRIAGE IS COUNTERCULTURAL

Couples today experience their lives as filled with things to do: people to meet, projects to finish, letters to write, calls to make, or appointments to keep. . . . The strange thing, however, is that it is very hard not to be busy. Being busy provides a certain status. . . . Being busy and being important often seem to mean the same thing. In some of the production-oriented societies being busy, having an occupation, has become one of the main ways that people have of identifying themselves.

By contrast, people in the eastern part of my country learn to slow down. They appreciate the present moment and take time to be present to others and enjoy their company. Their poverty thus strengthens their faith, patience, and relationships with others.

The "me first" mentality. We are a nation of individualists being told, "You deserve a break today," "We do it all for you," and "You're worth it." We read magazines with titles like *Self* to reinforce our attention to our rights and needs. This is not a good context for marriage, which involves self-sacrifice, unselfishness, and attention to the needs of others. And our increasingly sophisticated technology leaves us even more isolated from one another and engenders a detached-onlooker mentality — poor training for the intimacy that marriage requires.

An overemphasis on appearances. Although we live in a world of artificial flavors, colors, and textures, we tend to pretend that our artificial surroundings are real. We want everything to look good — instead of real. In a "Peanuts" cartoon, Lucy asks her brother, Linus, to get her a dish of ice cream, adding, "Mint! Make sure it's mint!!" When he comes back with a scoop of green ice cream, she comments that it doesn't taste like mint. Linus admits, "All we had was vanilla, but you can do amazing things with a green felt tip pen." Our focus on appearances can too easily color our approach to relationships, which aren't always as neat and perfect as we would like.

The illusion of control. We benefit from technology that makes our lives more comfortable. But technology also has a downside. It focuses our attention on *how* we do things rather than on *why* we want to do them. It also fosters the illusion that we can control what happens. We can be afflicted with overconfidence in our abilities to shape our lives, a sense that we can — and will — do it all and that we don't need God in our lives. But we can't do it all, and we do need God.

A lack of attachment. Americans value the novel, the new, the different. When something wears out, replace it. Move on. What's true for cameras, toothbrushes, and contact lenses is too often true for jobs, homes, values, and marriages. Permanence and attachment are suspect. It's better, we think, to find a new partner than to do the work necessary to make a good life with the partner we have.

A GOOD MARRIAGE IS COUNTERCULTURAL

In the face of all this, it's no wonder you might think that the odds are against the possibility of a lasting marriage. You may even be right — unless you take some bold steps.

One of these bold steps is clear: hard work. Marriage today requires harder work than marriages in the past. Although common sense, a good heart, and natural abilities are important, they are insufficient. To overcome the obstacles our culture throws in our path, we need careful preparation, new skills, and systematic attention to the marital relationship. What follows in this book is an effort to show you the skills you need.

But an honest look at the cultural context of marriage today leads to another conclusion: a successful marriage today must be countercultural. You and your spouse must strive — and work — to live differently than the people around you. Marital success and happiness lie in the reversing of the values and habits of our society — in living simply instead of acquiring more things, in being rather than doing, in putting others before yourself, in embracing the messiness of life rather than focusing on appearances, in relinquishing the illusion of control, and in treasuring what lasts rather than lusting after the new.

The Countercultural Marriage

These ideas are not entirely new. But there's a difference today. In the past, the tasks, attitudes, and skills involved

6

in growing up were more congenial to marital stability. Social institutions were more likely to provide the support young couples needed. Now young people must create the support they need. They accept the values of a materialistic, individualistic, secular culture at their peril. In fact, they need to take a conscious stance of opposition to lifestyles and values of the people around them.

What does a countercultural marriage look like? Here are some ideas about it that you might find helpful:

Simplify. Today it seems that we have the resources to satisfy virtually every conceivable need and desire. It's important to make some distinctions between the two. We desire many things. Which of them are needs? Which can we do without? What price will we pay to satisfy desires for things we can do without?

I am not advocating radical poverty for everyone. Our lives are enriched by the dazzling array of goods and services our economy makes available to us — music and art, travel and good food, books and computers, comfortable homes and many other things. But we need to be selective about what we choose. In particular, we need to be careful about slipping into a consumerist lifestyle where our time and energy are squandered in the pursuit of things.

Simplify. Just say no. Shop at a secondhand store even if you can afford to shop at the mall. Spend a night at home instead of out on the town. Slow down. In the midst of all that is in motion around us, it takes energy and courage to intentionally do less and be more.

As John Kavanaugh, S.J., points out in his wonderful book entitled *Following Christ in a Consumer Society: The Spirituality of Cultural Resistance,* this is not "good news for business":

> Let us suppose that you are a married person with children. If you are relatively happy with your life, if you enjoy spending time with your children, playing with them and talking with them; if you like nature, if you enjoy sitting in your yard or on your front steps, if your sexual life is relatively happy, if you have a peaceful sense of who you are and are stabilized in your relationships, if you like to pray in solitude, if you just like talking to people, visiting them, spending time in conversation with them, if you enjoy living simply, if you sense no need to compete with your friends or neighbors — *what good are you economically* in terms of our system? You haven't spent a nickel yet.

Give — and receive. Marriage and family life require unselfishness — a truly countercultural virtue in our individualistic culture. Cultivate an attitude of care and concern for others. Look for opportunities to serve. Set aside the fear that an unselfish concern for others will somehow diminish you. It won't. To the contrary, generosity causes us to grow. In the words of the prayer attributed to Saint Francis, "It is in giving that we receive."

Embrace messiness and imperfection. We aren't perfect. If we don't learn this lesson before we are married, married life will teach it in a hurry. Even so, many people persist in the illusion that perfection is a reasonable goal. They believe that they can force life to conform to an ideal pattern if only they work at it hard enough. This is a prescription for chronic frustration — and, often, catastrophic disappointment. It's far better to acknowledge and accept the truth that we don't control our lives. If we do, we can turn to the One who does.

Acknowledge the grace of God. God is in control. God's ways are often mysterious; we surely don't understand all that befalls us and those we love. But we can have confidence in God's grace. When we lose sight of it, the burdens of the world lie heavily on us. When we are conscious of God's love and presence in our lives, we can bear all things in the assurance that we have what we need.

Believe that forever is possible. Confidence in God's grace gives us the assurance that we can enter into a marriage that lasts. Forever *is* possible. Our commitment to our spouse in marriage gives us a solid foothold in a world that prizes the new, the novel, and the disposable.

These are some of the attitudes that will serve couples like Jason and Marie well as they contemplate marriage. If they choose these values, they will be living their married lives

9

within the culture we have. In many ways, they will look a lot like everyone else. They will work at normal jobs, shop at the mall, have dates on Saturday night. When they have children, they will probably trade in their sporty compact car for a van.

But they will think about their married lives in ways that are different from the ways others think. Their values will contrast sharply with the values of the surrounding culture. Theirs will be a marriage that is lived within society as we know it, but in sharp opposition to it in fundamental ways.

To live this way is not easy. It requires a firm foundation in a way of life that is strong and tested and true. That brings us to the most radical countercultural idea of all — the Catholic Christian tradition of marriage.

The Catholic
Vision
of Marriage

Even though they grew up Catholic, it didn't occur to Jeremy and Amber to think that the Catholic Church had much useful to say about marriage. To them, Catholic teaching was a set of rules, do's and don'ts — with more don'ts than do's. However, they are thinking of getting married, and they've been taking a look at what the Catholic Church says about it. They've read a booklet on the subject and liked what it said. The church's perspective on marriage seems to be refreshingly inspiring, respectful, and realistic, particularly in contrast to the popular images of marriage as filled with either passionate romance or boring routine. Jeremy and Amber are discovering more in their Catholic heritage than they thought was there — a long-term view of marriage and commitment, and a source of support for their life together.

A Catholic Christian view of marriage begins with a view of the human person as made for love. We are made in God's image — a God who is love — and we long for intimacy. The first chapter of Genesis describes this reality well: "God created humankind in his image, in the image of God he created them; male and female he created them" (1:27). We are made for one another, and this longing for intimacy, Genesis tells us, is part of being made in the image of God. Although the human being has many ways to meet this longing for intimacy, marriage is the most intense and powerful, the most inclusive experience of human relationship and intimacy.

It means that God made us to love each other. Marriage is not a human invention, a convenience, a social contract, or a cultural institution. It's a state of life that speaks to the deepest truths about us.

The Bible actually gives two different accounts of the creation of the sexes, in the first and second chapters of Genesis. In the first chapter, besides learning that our maleness and femaleness — together — reflect God's image, we are told to have children and form families. The second chapter of Genesis, which we will look at more in the chapter "Skill Nine: Grow in the Spiritual Life" (page 131), says that marriage is good for us; it is where we find suitable partners for ourselves.

The Catholic Church teaches that there are two purposes to marriage. One is the companionship of the partners themselves, a source of grace and joy and fulfillment. The other is the purpose of having children.

These two ends of marriage are complementary. Having children is one of the joys that bless the union of husband and wife. The love of the partners for each other is naturally expressed in the children they have together. In the past, the two ends of marriage were contrasted with each other. Today, the church prefers to emphasize how they are interconnected; the Second Vatican Council called marriage "an intimate communion of life and love." We will look at this in more detail in the chapters "Skill Nine: Grow in the Spiritual Life" (page 131) and "Skill Ten: Be Open to Being a Parent" (page 153).

The Catholic vision of marriage sees marriage as a *vocation* — a calling. Another way of talking about a vocation is as God's dream for us. God is intimately involved in it. The dimensions of this calling reach deeply into our hearts. They touch the most basic sense of who we are.

In their excellent book titled *Marrying Well: Possibilities in Christian Marriage Today,* Evelyn and James Whitehead describe a vocation as

> an invitation into my own identity as a Christian. It
> is an invitation that takes shape both in my deepest
> hopes and dreams and in the challenges offered me by
> the significant people in my life. It is the particular way
> I find myself called to love, to care for the world and to
> witness to Christian faith. A vocation is not an authori-

tative decree visited upon me from outside. It is rather *who I am*, trying to happen.

Something this important is not entered into lightly. It's also worth preparing for carefully. Think about the years of training necessary to enter a profession or even to learn a craft. Your marriage is more important than any career and requires careful thought, prayer, discernment, and continual work.

Marriage Is a Sacrament

In addition to seeing marriage as a high calling, a vocation, the Catholic tradition also sees it as a sacrament. A line from the *Catechism of the Catholic Church* describes sacraments as "efficacious signs of grace, instituted by Christ and entrusted to the church, by which divine life is dispensed to us."

What does it mean to say that marriage is a sacrament? There's much to say about this. In fact, I will devote a good portion of the chapter "Skill Nine: Grow in the Spiritual Life" (page 131) to discussing it in more detail. Here I want to make just a couple of basic points.

Sacraments are *signs* of God's love. They are concrete, visible manifestations of things that are invisible and intangible. As Christians, we know that God loves us and is personally involved in our lives in many ways. Sacraments allow us to grab hold of what God does for us in concrete

THE CATHOLIC VISION OF MARRIAGE

ways. We can see, touch, taste God's intimate involvement in our lives.

Marriage is a visible sign — to the spouses and to others — of the lifelong, faithful love of God. As the spouses experience between themselves a love and acceptance far beyond what they could imagine or hope for, and as others see their love for each other, God's love is evident. In effect, they are telling their family and friends and associates, "Do you want to know how deeply and even passionately God loves you? Then watch the way we love each other and delight in each other's presence. That's just a hint of the wonderful love God has for all of us every minute of every day."

Here's how several couples I know describe God's presence in their marriage:

It's like Christ is a third partner in our marriage, as invested in the success of our marriage as we are.

It's not all up to us. God is in our relationship with us — although we need to try as hard as we can to make our marriage work.

God is with us, not just on our wedding day, but every day, whether it's taking out the garbage or deciding what's for dinner. We know that our faith is a part of how we live and care for each other for the rest of our lives.

These words hint at an even deeper mystery about the sacramental sign of Christian marriage. The love and unity of the man and wife in marriage is a sign of unity of Christ and his church. Love and unity are the whole purpose of our lives. God is a Trinity of three Persons — Father, Son, and Holy Spirit — living in perfect love and unity. We cannot achieve this perfection in our marriages, but a Christian marriage nevertheless contains within it something of the dazzling beauty of God's cosmic plan for human beings. It says, "Come, look. God is here."

Sacraments are more than signs of God's grace. They *are* God's grace. In the theological language of the church, sacraments are signs that actually bring about the reality they signify. The water of baptism doesn't simply symbolize divine cleansing from sin and rebirth into new life with God. The water actually accomplishes this spiritual cleansing. So too with the bread and wine of the Eucharist. They signify God's life-giving nourishment, but they also are real food and real drink for our famished spirits.

So too for marriage. It's a sign of God's love. It also brings about God's love.

This has wonderful practical implications. The sacramental nature of marriage means that we can draw on a strength beyond our own in the daily stresses and strains of our lives together. God's grace is available to us in our problems and difficulties. The very nature of marriage means that God is with us always.

In *Marriage: Sacrament of Hope and Challenge*, William Roberts puts it this way:

Christian marriage does not reveal this love of Christ merely in the sense of pointing it out and reminding us of it. The sacrament of marriage *makes Christ's love present.* Through the mutual exchange of love between wife and husband, Christ manifests his presence to the couple and enriches them with the gift of love. (italics added)

Christian marriage is sometimes called a school of love. Because Christ is really and truly present in it, this is a school where real learning takes place. The spouses will learn what real love is throughout their lives. They will learn about generosity and forgiveness, about forbearance and sacrifice, about dying and new life. When children come, the lessons in the school of love expand. They will learn to live for others in feeding the baby at 2 A.M., in working to pay for the mortgage and clothing and tuition, in driving to soccer games, in guiding children through the storms of adolescence. Others will look to their marriage and see a sign of Christ's self-sacrificing love. The spouses will each experience Christ's love because they have freely chosen to live their lives together.

That is why the husband and wife administer the sacrament of marriage to each other. Other sacraments are administered by the priest or bishop. But the priest or deacon is only a witness to the sacrament of marriage. The essence of the sacrament is the exchange of vows. The church can bless it and recognize it, but only the couple can make these promises.

THE CATHOLIC VISION OF MARRIAGE

The Catholic tradition emphasizes three qualities of the wedding vows: marriage is *lifelong, exclusive,* and *indissoluble.*

Marriage is *lifelong.* That is, the bride and groom promise to share the rest of their lives with each other. It is *exclusive* — an intimate life with the other person and only the other person. It is *indissoluble* — a bond that lasts until death.

A man and woman who freely promise this kind of bond with each other share in the very life of God. Even more, the grace of God enters their lives, equipping them to meet the challenges of marriage, strengthening them, consoling them, leading them ever more deeply into the joys of a life together.

Jeremy and Amber have grown more thoughtful as they learn about the Catholic vision of marriage. They think that entering into a lifelong, exclusive, indissoluble bond that reflects the nature of God is a serious matter indeed. They hadn't thought about it that way before, and at times, they are a bit intimidated by how daunting it all looks.

On the other hand, the Catholic vision of marriage, solemn as it might be, looks attractive. The aspects of marriage that look intimidating are also inspiring. It doesn't seem wise to think about their vows as anything other than lifelong, exclusive, and indissoluble. After all, that is the kind of marriage they want to have.

Catholic marriage is inspiring to them in another way. It looks like a vision of marriage with enough depth and strength to prevail in the face of the cultural pressures that tear so many marriages apart. If marital success depends on being different, they think, it seems like a good idea to have the power of God on their side.

Jeremy and Amber need skills as well as vision. The rest of this book will discuss the skills they need:

- a knowledge of themselves as people loved by God and as unique individuals;
- an understanding of what real love is and a capacity for personal intimacy;
- a personal maturity, including accurate life assumptions, a clear set of values, and a capacity for commitment and responsibility;
- an understanding of how their families of origin will affect their marriage;
- an ability to communicate and listen effectively;
- an awareness of how gender and role issues can affect a marriage;
- a comfort with their own sexuality, and their partner's;
- a knowledge of how expectations about money and work affect marriage;
- a firm grounding in spirituality;
- an openness to the skills and growth involved in parenting;
- an appreciation of marriage as a process.

Our first marriage skill looks at our self-esteem. We know that God loves us. But how much do we love ourselves?

THE CATHOLIC VISION OF MARRIAGE

Skill: *I know myself well as loved by God, I like who I am, and I am comfortable with times of solitude.*

Learn to Love Yourself

Heather and Jason have gone together for two years. Jason is beginning to feel smothered because Heather doesn't want to do anything without him — and she doesn't want him to do anything without her. Heather wants Jason's opinion about everything; she doesn't do anything without his approval. Heather panics at the thought that they might break up. Whenever Jason mentions his concerns about their relationship, Heather assumes that he must be right and intensifies her efforts to please him. She is determined to make herself into the person she thinks is perfect for Jason. Heather's friends are tired of hearing about what Jason thinks, what Jason does, and what the two of them are doing together.

Jason is getting pretty tired of this too. "Who *is* Heather?" he wonders. "Does she have a life apart from me? Is she just an extension of me?" Jason is right to be troubled by this part of their relationship. Something very basic isn't quite right.

Strong and satisfying marriages begin with the self, the individual. In a committed and long-lasting relationship, what you think of me and what I think of you are obviously critical components. More important, however, is what *I* think of *me*.

When we hear Jesus, through the pages of Scripture, telling us to love our neighbors *as ourselves,* do we really know what it means to love ourselves? Do we know how to regard ourselves with a healthy objectivity that can name our own personal strengths and weaknesses? Can we make choices for ourselves that, while respecting the worth and dignity of others, are for our own well-being? This is the nature of loving ourselves. This is healthy self-esteem. And this is the beginning of a great marriage.

Unfortunately, our society finds it hard to recognize and appreciate healthy self-esteem. For example, there are those who wonder how one can merge a healthy self-esteem with sound values such as sacrifice, hard work, and service. Such values and a healthy self-esteem would seem to be mutually exclusive — but they're not. The person who works long, hard hours to support a family, who is invested in the community, and who is available to lend a helping hand to a neighbor can have a well-grounded and healthy self-esteem. The fact is, healthy self-esteem frees one to be a great lover — so self-sacrifice and service are usually signs of high self-esteem.

LEARN TO LOVE YOURSELF

But what about those people who seem conceited, self-centered, and egotistical? Do they have too much self-esteem? And how are they different from those who feel genuinely good about themselves and display a strong sense of self-confidence?

In *Your Child's Self-Esteem,* a classic among parenting books, Dorothy Corkille Briggs observes that "high self-esteem is not a noisy conceit. It is a quiet sense of self-respect, a feeling of self-worth. When you have it deep inside, you're glad you're you. Conceit is but a whitewash to cover low self-esteem. With high self-esteem you don't waste time and energy impressing others; you already know you have value." In other words, people who appear to overvalue themselves may, deep inside, feel exactly the opposite.

Briggs also offers a clear definition of what self-esteem is: very simply, self-esteem is how one feels about oneself. Good, or healthy, self-esteem, she maintains, is the conviction that we are lovable and worthwhile, a belief that is built on the reactions of people close to us when we're young. Briggs explains how those people function as mirrors to the growing person. If those mirrors are warped or negative, she contends, we erect defenses, withdraw, submit to a self-effacing life, or react with a combination of these responses.

One way to see how self-esteem affects a relationship is to watch poor self-esteem at work. Let's look at Heather and Jason's relationship again. Heather is not sure of who she is and whether she is really OK. As she grew fond of Jason early

LEARN TO LOVE YOURSELF

in their relationship, she gave away parts of herself, defining herself, to a large degree, as "Jason's girlfriend." Without a clear sense of her own self and her own boundaries, Heather easily takes Jason's opinions as better or right, rather than asking herself, "What do I think about this?" With her evident low self-esteem, Heather may even be setting herself up for abuse, should she meet someone who does not treat her with respect.

Heather lacks two basic skills essential to a healthy relationship. In an article titled "Making Marriage Work: 'Being in Love' Is Not Enough" (*St. Anthony Messenger,* November 1982), psychologist Michael E. Cavanagh sees an authentic sense of self-esteem as the first of seven skills necessary for a successful marriage. His second skill is closely related to the first: a *clear, strong, flexible* sense of self. With a clear, strong, and flexible sense of self, I am able to be in a healthy relationship with another. Heather lacks an authentic sense of self-esteem and does not have a clear, strong, flexible sense of herself.

For example, with a *clear* sense of self, Heather would know who she is and what she needs to grow and flourish as an individual. She would value a certain amount of freedom for herself, and she would respect Jason's freedom. She would seek out people who relate to her with respect and affection. Without a clear sense of self, Heather lets herself be molded by others, especially Jason. She is not concerned about the respect others have for her.

With a *strong* sense of self, Heather would not allow anyone to restrict who she is or how she wishes to grow. She would have a strong set of basic values that define who she is. Her life choices would be well grounded in those basic values. Without a strong sense of self, Heather repeatedly defers to Jason and disregards her own needs, emotions, or opinions.

With a *flexible* sense of self, Heather would be willing to temper her own needs for Jason's equally valid needs. She would appreciate the need to compromise so that Jason's needs, as well as the needs of the relationship, might be met. Without a flexible sense of self, Heather's rigid limitations are suffocating Jason — and their relationship.

Elements of Healthy Self-Esteem

What does a healthy self-esteem look like? What are some of its qualities? How can I recognize healthy self-esteem in others? Most important, how can I tell if I have a healthy self-esteem? People with healthy self-esteem can make the following statements about themselves with honesty and confidence:

- *I am good.* God saw that humans were "very good" — as opposed to merely "good," like the fruits of creation on previous days. So, I am very good. I am made in God's image, a reflection of the knowing, loving, gentle Presence at the heart of the universe. And, as they say, "God doesn't make junk." Knowing I am good, I respect myself and expect respect from others. I do not allow myself to be abused — and I don't abuse myself. I don't judge my own value by how others treat me, either positively or negatively. The psalmist captures it perfectly for us: "I praise you, for I am fearfully and wonderfully made" (Psalm 139:14).

- *I am a gift.* Although I know that I can develop — or refuse to develop — certain talents or abilities that I naturally have, I know that I am not the source of those special faculties. I know that's God's department. I didn't earn the gifts and abilities I have; they are gifts to me, which make me a gift to others. My job is to rejoice in and enjoy what I have been given and to share those gifts with others. I am filled to overflowing with God's love, and the only limitation to how much love I experience is my openness to God.

- *I am not perfect.* I am only too aware of my limitations, but I choose not to focus on them. Rather, I know I can learn from my shortcomings. I know that my weaknesses are as God-given as my strengths and that they can teach me a great deal — about myself and about human nature. Because of my weaknesses, I am more compassionate and patient with others who, like me, are not perfect.

- *I am worth spending time with.* I enjoy spending time with myself. I like to dream, create, wonder, and ponder. I like to think my own thoughts in the company of myself.

LEARN TO LOVE YOURSELF

I also take time for myself so that I can grow to be more fully myself and thus give more to others. I know, too, that others enjoy my company — most of the time — but I don't judge my worth by how others treat me. When I am not welcome, for example, I do not assume that it's me; rather, it has to do with circumstances.

- *Every aspect of who I am is good.* Although I can misuse them, all parts of me are good. God made them all to be good: my body, my feelings, my intelligence, my conscience, my faith, and my sexuality. As a person with healthy self-esteem, I nourish and develop every part of me as much as possible, and I appreciate how interconnected my various parts are in the whole person that is me.

- *I am not merely what I do or what I have or what I look like.* I recognize our culture's tendency to define and value me according to external standards, but I know that I am so much more than what is on the surface. The real treasure of me is far deeper than what I accomplish, what I have, or what I look like.

- *I am free to love.* I am not afraid to give others the "safeties" that Dorothy Corkille Briggs says we all need: the gifts of trust, nonjudgment, empathy, and a sense of being cherished in a way that promotes unique growth. My relational energies are not caught up in my own emotional black hole, where I spend my time and energies wondering what people think of me, looking for

LEARN TO LOVE YOURSELF

ways to feel better about myself, and trying to win the high regard of others. My family and friends benefit because of my healthy self-esteem.

Especially important to a person with high self-esteem is the experience of solitude. Solitude is different from loneliness. In both cases, I feel alone. The difference is, I choose solitude and, in all likelihood, do not choose loneliness. Everyone who loves someone is sometimes lonely, but if my self-esteem is strong, this feeling of loneliness does not cause me anxiety. When I feel good about myself, I will not only want to spend some time by myself; I will value that time. I know that solitude renews and deepens my sense of myself and gives me more of my goodness to share with others. Again and again, Jesus sought the solitude of the desert, knowing that he would return to those he loved with greater passion.

Low-Self-Esteem Cover-Ups

Low self-esteem leaves me frightened of the world around me, although I may not admit it. When I don't value myself, I don't see any reason for the world to value me either. No one and no place is safe, for everywhere I turn, I see and hear criticisms, judgments, and high expectations. In order to survive, I look for ways to cope.

- *I put on a mask.* My mask reflects back to you what I expect you're looking for. The problem is, maintaining the mask calls for a great deal of energy. I have to be on constant alert for signals — from you, others, and the surrounding culture — that will tell me what and who I'm supposed to be. In the meantime, the real me gets lonely — and lost. I risk beginning to believe the mask myself.

- *I become envious and jealous.* I look at others and decide that I want what they have; I want to be who they are — because they're obviously better than I am. The cancer of envy and jealousy can eat away at me until I've become a mean-spirited, cynical person. My own low self-esteem may drive me to the point of discrediting the worth of others.

- *I settle for less than I deserve.* When I don't value myself, I certainly don't expect you to value me. As a result, I will let you treat me in ways that may be degrading and abusive. I will not care enough about myself to get out of situations or relationships that are harmful.

- *I need power.* Since I don't consider myself of any worth, I look for ways to claim power for myself — real or imaginary. With this power, I feel a certain entitlement to your admiration, but my sense of worth comes only at the cost of your powerlessness. Ironically, I may try to gain a sense of power by playing the role of a helpless and powerless victim. As you reach out to help me, I feel some control — power — over the relationship.

LEARN TO LOVE YOURSELF

- *I need to continuously impress others.* I become obsessed with my looks, my accomplishments, or my possessions. I may go to financial extremes to gather around myself whatever I think it will take not only to get your attention but also to leave you impressed.

- *I live through others or cling too tightly.* Because I consider my own life to be worthless, I look to experience life through others. I may even try to lead your life by making major decisions for you or by demanding that you keep me central to your life. When you fail to let me live my life through you, I simply try harder.

- *I blame others.* My low self-esteem can convince me that I'm not responsible for my own problems. Because I don't consider myself wise enough, strong enough, or smart enough to influence even my own life, then someone else must be responsible for my problems and my unhappiness. This often takes the form of "if only": "If only my parents hadn't . . ."; "If only the bank would have . . ."

- *I attempt to escape through various kinds of addictions.* Alcohol, drugs, food, work, gambling, hobbies — even the Internet: I look for those things that will keep me from being fully present to and with myself. Desperate to deaden the persistent pain of self-loathing, I look for those escapes that will leave me physically or mentally numb — or both.

Although attempts to cover up low self-esteem may make me feel better about myself in the moment, the "feel better" quality wears off quickly. Inevitably, I am left, once again, with the self I label unacceptable.

Can I Work on My Self-Esteem?

Low self-esteem is common in our culture. In an article titled "Gentleness" (*Praying,* November/December 1993), Gerald May comments on just how hard most people are on themselves:

> In my experience as a psychiatrist and as a human being, the deepest, most pervasive pathology I have seen is the incredible harshness we have toward ourselves. I don't know where it comes from originally, but I know it is at the core of so many of our troubles. We jerk ourselves around, berate ourselves, drive ourselves and confine ourselves in ways we would never subject an animal to. . . . Some of us are meaner than others, but I have yet to meet a person in modern western culture who was not in some way cruelly self-abusive.

Given May's observations, what can we do to build a lasting, healthy self-esteem?

The paradox is, self-esteem is a by-product, not a direct goal. If we set out to feel better about ourselves, we're likely to end up more focused on and frustrated with ourselves than before. In her book *Gently Lead*, Polly Berrien Berends comments, "Real self-esteem is not a matter of thinking well of oneself but of being what one really is."

A self-directed campaign to improve my self-esteem will accomplish very little. Rather, if I take a gentle and appreciative look at how I go through my days, I will see the many ways in which I care and love more deeply than I may be aware of. I will see the main obstacles I've overcome, and I will appreciate the better person I am for having faced those challenges. I can see my strengths and successes in loving others and in pursuing what I care most deeply about. I see the daily wonders of myself that I can easily miss when I focus on my failures and shortcomings.

It's a simple matter of seeing my full self and appreciating the fine qualities I see. The result is my own healthier self-esteem and the energy to help others appreciate themselves more.

A healthy self-esteem is not a question of choosing between loving others or loving myself but a matter of loving myself so that I can love others more fully and freely, with all my heart. Knowing that I am loved by God, I can love God in return with all that I am. I can follow the law of love.

When Jesus was asked to name the greatest commandment of the law, he named two. Number one was to love the Lord your God with all your heart, and with all your soul, and with all your mind, and with all your strength. Number two was to love your neighbor as yourself.

LEARN TO LOVE YOURSELF

Apply Jesus' lesson to your marriage. Love your spouse as yourself. Love him, love her, with the same warmth, generosity, respect, and commitment that you have for your own self. Loving the other person begins with *you*.

Once *you* are in order, you can turn your attention to loving the person who shares your life. That's the second skill, and there's much to learn about it.

For Reflection

1. *How do I see good self-esteem as being important to healthy relationships?*

2. *Who do I know who has strong self-esteem? What in their behaviors and attitudes displays their strong self-esteem?*

3. *Who do I know who has poor self-esteem? What defenses — wearing a mask, becoming envious and jealous, settling for less than they deserve, needing power, needing to impress others, living through others or clinging too tightly, blaming others, or attempting to escape through various kinds of addictions — do I see at work in them? Is there anything I can do to help encourage better self-esteem in these people?*

4. *What does solitude mean to me? If I had a day to myself in solitude, how would I spend it?*

5. *How do I understand the connection between loving God, loving others, and loving myself?*

LEARN TO LOVE YOURSELF

Skill: *I understand*
what real love is and have
a capacity for personal intimacy.

Let Others Get Close

Even though Jennifer has been dating Rob for three years, she doesn't think she really knows him. Rob occasionally tells Jennifer that he loves her, usually after they've been in a social situation in which he is especially proud of being with her. He's comfortable talking about sports, their friends, and what they're going to do together. He doesn't have much to say about himself. When Jennifer asks him about how he feels or what he believes, Rob shrugs off the question with "Whatever" and changes the subject. Jennifer wonders what Rob means when he tells her he loves her.

Jennifer thinks she loves Rob, but when she senses this barrier between them, she wonders whether she really is in love with him. Their feelings for each other have taken them to a certain point in their relationship. Now something more is needed.

Love is a major word in our culture. It's a very loose term. We use the word *love* to talk about our reactions to everything from hairstyles to cars to television programs. Our culture offers a surplus of movies, books, and songs about love — much of it powerful and inspiring. But what do we really mean when we say, "I love," and what don't we mean?

We know that marriages, historically, weren't always based on love — and still aren't today in some cultures. In our culture, however, love is foundational to a healthy marriage.

But is love primarily a feeling or is it an action, a decision? Is it, perhaps, a bit of both? In the comic strip titled "For Better or For Worse," by Lynn Johnston, the teenage daughter remarks to a friend, "Isn't it amazing, Dawn, how, in one night, your whole life can change? We walked all the way home from the movie, holding hands. It was snowing . . . so slightly. Then he kissed me under the street lamp on 5th Street — and suddenly I felt as if it was summertime! Now my stomach is in knots. I can't think about anything but him. I keep going over everything we said to each other. Is this what love is really like?" Dawn wisely responds, "I'm not sure, but I think that's how it starts out."

If love starts with these feelings, is that where it ends? If I no longer feel a certain way toward a person, does that mean I no longer love that person?

The question of what love is has been grappled with by many a thinker, but it is more than just a theoretical question. If I say, "I love you," and I mean something completely different from what you mean when you say the same thing to me, we may have a big problem.

Many authors draw a distinction between *falling in love*—a strong state of feeling—and *real love.* In his best-selling book *The Road Less Traveled,* M. Scott Peck defines love as "the will to extend one's self for the purpose of nurturing one's own or another's spiritual growth." He points out that real love starts where feelings may wane or change, at the point where we need to decide whether we are willing to extend ourselves for the good of the other, a good that is directly linked to our own growth.

If love is more than a feeling, then do we learn to love or are we born knowing how to love? Most writers would say that we learn to love based on what we see and how we are loved. In his book *The Art of Loving,* psychoanalyst Erich Fromm talks about loving as an art, a skill that is difficult to practice well in our society, where *having* is valued over *being.*

The Love We Learn

In the foreword to *Loving Relationships: Self, Others, and God,* an excellent book on love by Robert Shelton, David W. Augsberger notes that some of the ways we are taught to love are flawed and incomplete, leaving us with warped ideas about love. He says that "the love we learn is often more confusing than calming, more complex than simple, more ambivalent than constant, more distorted than direct. Often the love

37

learned is only a fragment of an authentic loving relationship enlarged to become everything, a part pretending to be the whole." Augsberger describes these incomplete ideas of love in the following terms. I suggest you use the question following each description to consider how it may apply in your life.

- "Love is control: If you love me you will do what I want and act as I prescribe." *(Do I try to have too much power over you?)*

- "Love is agreement: If you love me you will not differ from my position because to differ is to reject." *(Do I expect constant harmony from you?)*

- "Love is understanding: If you love me you will know what I need or want without my telling or asking." *(Do I expect you to read my mind?)*

- "Love is conformity: If you love me your behavior will fit perfectly with everyone around you." *(Do I expect you to fit perfectly with my friends and family?)*

- "Love is obligation: If you love me you owe me your loyalty, and respect for me is your duty." *(Do I expect you to give me respect without my earning it?)*

- "Love is denial: If you love me you will hear no evil, see no evil, say no evil about me." *(Do I expect you to never see my faults?)*

LET OTHERS GET CLOSE

- "Love is anxiety: If you love me you will be anxious when I am anxious, feel the fears I feel." *(Do I expect you to see the world exactly the way I do?)*

- "Love is rescuing: If you love me you will let me dedicate my life to rescuing, saving, taking care of your dependency needs." *(Do I expect you to need me as unhealthily as I may need you?)*

- "Love is closeness: If you love me you will always be close, you will never act, feel, or be distant." *(Do I expect you to be an extension of me?)*

- "Love is availability: If you love me you will always be present, open, willing to match my schedule." *(Do I expect you to be on my time schedule?)*

Notice how conditional each of these incomplete ideas of love is. I will love you *only if* you conform on my terms to what I need. But this isn't love. Rather, this kind of conditional relating actually blocks growth and genuine love. To the extent that these are part of one's past experience or present habits of love, they need a critical examination.

There are, however, many kinds of complete love that can help us learn about the love on which marriage is built. We might look at these loves as ingredients that, when mixed with our full life experiences, help us prepare for marriage by fashioning our notions of what love is — and what it isn't.

In *Marrying Takes a Lifetime,* H. Paul LeMaire suggests that there are at least three such loves: parental love, friendship, and romantic love.

Parental love is our first experience of being loved. At its best, parental love is a self-sacrificing love that is generous, unselfish, faithful, and long suffering — qualities needed in marital love as well. If self-fulfillment is one's only focus in marriage, then the needs of the other will be seen as a threat rather than as an opportunity to care.

Friendship is another form of love that has much to teach us. Friendship is a mutual love. I'll never forget the day my middle son came home from kindergarten delighted that another child was his friend and he was that child's friend. My oldest son, at age twenty-one, has a best friend who shares with him his passion for mountain biking. At any age, friendship is a wondrous experience. It is marked by perseverance, a deepening self-knowledge, and a quiet and calm appreciation for the other — all critical to a healthy and satisfying marriage.

Romantic love — those strong feelings and attractions — also speaks to us of the love that grounds marriage. Romantic love shows us how we can be swept up into feelings about the other. Marital love certainly involves these kinds of strong emotions.

These three kinds of love — parental love, friendship, and romantic love — can help form the love we learn if we are open to their wisdom.

Lessons of Love

The Little Prince, by Antoine de Saint-Exupèry, a delightful children's book that is really for adults, teaches some valuable lessons about love. The little prince, who lives on a planet not much bigger than a house, travels from planet to planet asking everyone he meets about the meaning of life. Specifically, he wonders about friendship and his relationship with a rose back on his own planet. When he comes to Earth he meets a fox who asks the prince to tame him, which, the fox explains, means to establish ties. The fox elaborates:

> To me, you are still nothing more than a little boy who
> is just like a hundred thousand other little boys. And
> I have no need of you. And you, on your part, have no
> need of me. To you, I am nothing more than a fox like
> a hundred thousand other foxes. But if you tame me,
> then we shall need each other. To me, you will be unique
> in all the world. To you I shall be unique in all the world.

When the fox talks about the joys of taming, we hear the echoes of our own hearts:

> But if you tame me, it will be as if the sun came to
> shine on my life. I shall know the sound of a step that
> will be different from all the others. Other steps send
> me hurrying back underneath the ground. Yours will
> call me, like music, out of my burrow. And then look:
> you see the grain-fields down yonder? I do not eat

LET OTHERS GET CLOSE

bread. Wheat is of no use to me. The wheat fields have
nothing to say to me. And that is sad. But you have
hair that is the color of gold. Think how wonderful
that will be when you have tamed me! The grain, which
is also golden, will bring me back the thought of you.
And I shall love to listen to the wind in the wheat.

The little prince protests that he has much to do but not
much time, to which the fox replies, "One only understands
the things that one tames."

What does "taming," or being in a relationship, entail?
Love creates rituals, Saint-Exupéry explains. When the little
prince comes at a different time the next day to see the fox,
the talking animal tells him it would have been better to have
come at the same time so that, as the hour drew near, he
could be waiting and ready. The proper rites, the fox explains,
"are what make one day different from other days, one hour
from other hours."

But there is a cost. When the little prince is ready to
depart, the fox tells him that he will cry. But when the prince
concludes that it has done him no good at all, the fox says
that it has done him good because of the color of the wheat
fields. The fox then gives the little prince the gift of a three-
part secret:

It is only with the heart that one can see rightly; what
is essential is invisible to the eye.

LET OTHERS GET CLOSE

It is the time you have wasted for your rose that
makes your rose so important.

You become responsible, forever, for what you have
tamed. You are responsible for your rose.

But Why Is Love So Hard?

If we know that love is important and can make us truly
happy, why do we find it so hard? Psychologist Michael E.
Cavanagh says that most of us, because of our individual
histories, love "with a limp." We have all known the pain
of being hurt or disappointed. Perhaps it was a simple crush
on someone; perhaps it was a deep loss or even abusive treat-
ment. Each of these experiences leaves scars — tender places
that we may not even be aware of, but which come into play
when we try to love. This history presses in on our current
relationships and makes it hard for us to take the risks that
real love calls for.

M. Scott Peck states that the reason we don't risk ourselves more is ultimately due to laziness, which, like Cavanagh,
he connects to fear. The vulnerability that love asks of us can
look like too high a price. We prefer to stay in our safe shells
where we can't be hurt. Sadly, those shells keep us from being
fully alive. As John Powell puts it in his gem of a book titled
Why Am I Afraid to Tell You Who I Am?, "If I tell you who I
am, you may not like who I am, and it's all that I have."

To "tell you who I am," however, means I am willing — despite my painful history, despite my fear — to risk intimacy, the bedrock of healthy marital love. Unfortunately, our culture understands *intimacy* as synonymous with *sex*. When I say that I have been intimate with someone, my listener usually assumes that I have been sexually active. But intimacy is much more than sex. Intimacy involves letting the other get so close that I open up my deepest self in a way that I reserve for very few in life.

Developmental psychologist Erik Erikson suggests that there are key tasks we center on during each part of our lives, tasks that we need to accomplish at that time or else we must go back later to finish. He describes intimacy as "the flexible strength for being close." He says that intimacy — as opposed to isolation — is our main task between eighteen and thirty years of age. This task is built on the prior stage of identity — as opposed to role confusion — which is the main developmental task in the teen years, twelve to eighteen.

According to Erikson, both these stages — and others that precede them — are ultimately built on a foundation of trust in the world around us, usually established in the first two years of life. If experiences early in life leave us unable to see the world as a reliable place, we naturally wonder if others are relating with us fairly and honestly. We may fear getting too close to others because of potential pain and disappointment — and that fear may inhibit us from sharing our deepest selves. Thus, until we can trust the world around us, our ability for intimacy is severely hindered.

Intimacy means mutual availability, vulnerability, trust, and openness — and involves our emotional, intellectual, spiritual, and sexual selves. All this is built on trust that comes from commitment, a topic we examine more in the chapter "Skill Eleven: Get Ready to Change and Grow" (page 165).

Skills build on skills. Healthy self-esteem allows us to risk opening ourselves in real intimacy when the time comes for our relationship to grow into a love that is beyond feelings. Now it's time for something else.

It's time to grow up.

For Reflection

1. *How would I define love? What have been some of my own key experiences of love?*
2. *Who has helped me learn to love? How?*
3. *How do I see others around me love "with a limp," based on their past experiences?*
4. *What past experiences have left me loving "with a limp"?*
5. *Who has tamed me and whom have I tamed? How?*

Skill: *I am personally mature.*
I have accurate life assumptions,
psychological autonomy and maturity,
a clear set of values and beliefs, and
an understanding of and capacity for
responsibility and commitment.

Grow Up

Caroline was getting serious about her boyfriend, Bill, and she was being criticized for it. Some of her girlfriends thought Bill wasn't enough fun. That, Caroline thought, meant that he didn't drink as much as they did and liked to get to bed before dawn. More serious were the objections from her parents. "After all," her mother said, "Bill wants to be a teacher, and teachers don't make very good salaries." Caroline thought that the real questions were whether Bill would be a good teacher and whether he would enjoy it. She thought the answer to both was yes. Caroline thought about Bill — and decided to make up her own mind about his fitness to be her husband.

Caroline is becoming a mature adult. The psychological term is *personal autonomy.* Throughout her young life, her values, deeds, and decisions have been heavily influenced by other people — friends and family, teachers and pastors. Now she's ready to strike out on her own. If she decides to marry Bill, she'll be acting contrary to the desires of some of the people closest to her. If so, that will be all right with her.

I frequently ask my students to list those qualities one must have to enter marriage successfully. Almost always, and usually very high on the list, is a quality like "being grown up enough to know what one is taking on." In other words, maturity.

What makes a person mature?

Psychologist Michael E. Cavanagh suggests seven skills necessary for a successful marriage. Those skills are as follows: an authentic sense of self-esteem; a clear, strong, flexible sense of self; accurate life assumptions; healthy psychosexual development; psychological autonomy; psychological maturity; and the ability to communicate effectively. We will examine three of these skills that deal with personal maturity: accurate life assumptions, psychological autonomy, and psychological maturity.

Accurate Life Assumptions

Each of us has a set of basic ideas about what life means. These theories of life are learned in childhood, reinforced in adolescence, and hidden deep within us as adults. They frame the way we see the world and how we react to what happens around us and to us. Sometimes these assumptions are accurate. Sometimes, however, they are quite inaccurate. For example:

- "Marriage will validate my worth and fill my sense of emptiness, loneliness, and purposelessness with meaning and satisfaction." This person will look to a spouse to do what he or she should have done personally long before marriage.

- "Getting is more important than giving" or "Giving is more important than getting." This person has a narrow and lopsided view of life and of what to expect of self and others. This view will severely distort expectations of self and others.

- "Life is supposed to be fun" or "Life is supposed to be difficult." This person will find exactly what he or she expects to find in life. The fact is, life is a bit of both.

Each of these assumptions can determine decisions and trigger behaviors that could spell problems for the individual and the couple. If Josh, for example, thinks that Debra will always find him absolutely wonderful, that he's finally going to have life just the way he wants it, and that life and relationships are about having fun, he's going to have a hard time adjusting to the realities of marriage and a family. His basic life assumptions are not accurate.

Psychological Autonomy

Psychological autonomy is the ability to be one's own person, not dependent on a particular person or group for security or satisfaction. With this skill one can enjoy spending time alone as well as with others. It allows one to see both the nurturing and the destructive aspects of any relationship and to make decisions about the relationship that respect the good of all involved. It equips one to make decisions after listening to and seriously considering input from others, including parents. Psychological autonomy is especially essential to a Catholic Christian marriage, where living an active and fruitful faith calls for a well-grounded sense of one's tremendous worth in the eyes of God.

Cavanagh observes, "Autonomous people are likely to choose a spouse based on sound reasoning and free choice; to make decisions based on the good of the relationship rather than external influences; and to free their spouse to grow toward self-actualization." He adds, "People who lack autonomy are likely to choose a spouse on the basis of fear or default; to make decisions based on the need to conform; to be obedient or to please; and to view their spouse as a crutch instead of a separate and free human being."

In his book *Illusion and Disillusion*, James Crosby gives us an interesting way of looking at psychological autonomy by discussing it in terms of dependency and using the shapes of the letters *A, H,* and *M. Dependence* is like the letter *A.*

Note how the leaning sides slant in toward each other with a short connecting bar between them. If one side is removed, the other side will topple. Dependency causes a relationship to look much like the *A*. Each person in the relationship has a weak sense of self as an individual. The relationship will remain stable as long as the partners lean in and against each other. If one should lose his or her balance in that leaning stance, however, the other will lose balance as well, and the relationship will become seriously unstable. Sharon and Phil have a relationship like this. They rarely do anything without the other. Phil knows nothing about their finances, and Sharon knows nothing about simple home maintenance.

The letter *H* demonstrates *independence,* with its two strong upright sides and a minimal connection in between. In a relationship, this might look like what Marriage Encounter calls "married singles": two people together, but not sharing much of themselves with each other. The narrow connection between them is short and shallow and involves only the incidentals of a shared life. Each may have a strong sense of individual identity, but their identity as a couple is weak. Paul and Anne, for example, chat briefly at the breakfast table each morning before they rush off for another day of work. They won't see each other again until near midnight, when they each get home from their respective after-work involvements, be that volunteering in church or civic organizations, meeting friends, or working out at the gym.

The letter *M* demonstrates *interdependence,* which involves both dependency and independence. Partners have a clear sense of themselves as dependent on each other — as displayed by the center lines of the *M* sloping in toward each other — thus giving their relationship a strong identity. At the same time, they experience a healthy independence — demonstrated by the outside legs that can stand by themselves — as they pursue their own individual interests and friendships. Sean and Belinda have their respective interests and activities, but they also make time — daily — to share what's really going on in their lives and to enjoy each other's company.

In a class paper, a student of mine commented on the difference between an *A* relationship of dependence and a healthier one:

> I definitely had an *A* relationship once. All I could think about was him and how much he would like for me to do this or wear that. I sought his opinion on all of the decisions I should have made for myself. I even started the application process to the college he wanted to go to, and we were planning to become Quaker missionaries to India. Thank goodness (in retrospect) we parted. After a great deal of soul-searching, I discovered I did not have much in common with him and later was able to have a healthier *M* relationship.

Psychological Maturity

"When people are psychologically immature," Cavanagh comments, "both the authenticity of their decision to marry and the likelihood of their growing in marriage are questionable." He distinguishes, however, between what he calls a developmental lag, when a person's maturity level is slightly behind his or her chronological age, and a developmental fixation, when a part of the personality has gotten stuck at a much earlier stage and needs professional help. Cavanagh identifies the following problem areas:

- *selfishness*: a focus on "what's in it for me" and a blindness to the needs of others — unless recognizing and meeting those needs serves a self-centered purpose;

- *unrealistic expectations:* a conviction that the spouse-to-be is the "most beautiful person in the world" and there will never be any problems or unhappiness;

- *a craving for attention and affection:* a need for continuous, unconditional love, or else sulking, punishing the partner, or seeking attention and affection from an inappropriate source results;

- *emotional inappropriateness:* under- or overresponding to emotional stimuli and using one's emotions to manipulate others;

- *low tolerance for frustration or stress:* not being willing to take "no" for an answer and getting agitated in the face of ordinary stress;

- *an inaccurate perception of reality:* not seeing circumstances and events with objectivity;
- *jealousy and possessiveness:* wanting to be the sole source of fulfillment and joy in the other's life and resenting it if not.

When these kinds of behavior are common, basic maturity may be lacking, and professional help may be necessary.

Cavanagh observes that engaged people often cannot hear the need to work on any of these issues. He says that the time to do so is before falling in love. He also suggests that there continues to be too much social pressure to marry, which at times may lead people to marry before they're ready. (His marriage-readiness list has a number of items in common with our list. See the skills review.)

Clear Values and Beliefs

Besides accurate life assumptions, psychological autonomy, and psychological maturity, we also need to have a clear set of life values and beliefs if we are to take on the commitment of marriage. We need to know which aspects of life are more important for us than others. Otherwise, nothing is truly important.

An example from my own marriage demonstrates this. I enjoy spending time in the outdoors, hiking and camping. The natural surroundings of the outdoors nurture my spirit.

My husband, Mitch, however, doesn't enjoy that kind of activity. If I insisted that Mitch join me in outdoor activities, regular battles would, no doubt, arise. As it is, I find ways to nurture myself outdoors, but my marriage doesn't depend on getting Mitch to hike and camp with me on a regular basis. We both agree on the crucial values — areas like simplicity of lifestyle, honesty, faith, creativity, and self-nurturing — and find ways to respect them within the marriage. This makes a big difference in our mutual satisfaction.

The values and beliefs of a Catholic Christian marriage will be grounded in, among other things, the gospel message of unselfish love. But whatever our beliefs are, if we do not share a significant measure of agreement on our most important values, we can expect a great deal of frustration through the years.

What are my key values, and how do I determine their importance to me? One way to check on our values is to look at how we spend our time and money. An examination of our calendar and our checkbook will give us strong clues about what is really important to us, rather than what we may say is important. For example, Jared talks about the importance of serving others and staying fit, but he spends a lot of time and money on the latest music and video games; he rarely gets much physical exercise. Kristen, on the other hand, exercises regularly and does a lot of volunteer work. In theory, it would appear that Jared and Kristen share two common values: service and fitness. But their day-to-day choices do not bear this out. If Jared and Kristen start to have a serious relationship, they may have trouble with how they spend their time and money together.

Responsibility and Commitment

Another aspect of personal maturity is responsibility and commitment. A commitment taken on by a person who cannot handle responsibility will not hold for long. One way to think about responsibility is to break the word apart to form a definition: responsibility is the *ability to respond* to what comes our way in life. A commitment is supported by the ability to respond.

We learn about responsibility in many ways. We learn responsibility within our families, for example, and in the care of pets. We learn responsibility by being part of an athletic team or a member of an organization. When we think beyond ourselves to the needs of others and are willing to extend ourselves for a greater good beyond our own, we know the meaning of commitment and the responsibilities inherent to it.

In the movie *The Wedding Singer,* the two main characters gauge the personal maturity of others by observing their willingness — or lack thereof — to give up a window seat on the airplane to someone who prefers it. It's a little thing, but it illustrates an attitude of generosity that can make a big difference in a marriage.

Unfortunately, thinking beyond our own needs and wants is not encouraged or fostered in our commercial culture. Yet, countercultural though it may be, such generosity and other-centeredness are essential to a Catholic Christian marriage.

The Right Person

With the qualities of personal maturity — accurate life assumptions, psychological autonomy, psychological maturity, a clear set of values and beliefs, a sound sense of responsibility, and an ability to commit to something bigger than ourselves — how do we know when the "right" person comes along? How is that person going to seem different from all the others? If we ask most married people how they knew that their spouse was "the one," most will respond with a smile and a comment to the effect that somehow they just knew.

Sources like the *Old Farmer's Almanac* give us colorful clues from folklore for finding the perfect mate, such as "Hard boil an egg, cut it in half, discard the yolk, and fill the egg halves with salt. Sit on something you have never sat on before, eat the egg, and walk to bed backwards. You will dream of your future mate." Although this and similar methods suggested by the almanac are more entertaining than reliable, they do tell us that finding the right match has been a human quest for centuries.

Then there's the twenty-eight-year-old bachelor who, according to a June 9, 1998, Associated Press news release, got tired of his friends asking him when he was going to get married. He began giving them a particular date. The only problem: no bride. Not to worry, however. On the day of the wedding, his friends chose one for him from among those women who had either enrolled on the young man's special Web site or attended his bridal-candidate mixer, at the end of which there was a vote. He did marry the winner, but seriously, were there any winners in this scenario? Only time will tell.

While questions about the right person have disturbed humankind throughout most of recorded history, I suggest that there is likely more than one right person to marry. Thus, the question is not, "Is this the 'right' person?" but, "Am *I* ready to be the 'right' person for someone when we meet?" This, of course, is connected to the characteristics of personal maturity that we discussed earlier: accurate life assumptions, psychological autonomy, psychological maturity, clear values and beliefs, responsibility, and a capacity to commit to another.

Many of us have met people who, if the timing had been different, might have been right for us. But one or both of us were not ready for the commitment that marriage is — and the moment passed.

Is God involved in the finding of that other person? Definitely! Grace builds on nature. As we work on being the right person — healthy in the ways discussed in this book — God brings that person into our lives, if that is how we are called to live.

If Caroline decides that Bill is the right person for her, this mature choice is likely to bring her into conflict with her parents — possibly serious conflict. Many of you will find similar issues as you grow up and grow into marriage. Our families of origin have great influence on us. The skills to understand and deal with our families is the next item in our tool kit.

For Reflection

1. *What qualities do I need, and does my partner need, to be ready for marriage?*
2. *Of these, which qualities are the most important to me? Why?*
3. *Which qualities are not especially important to me? Why?*
4. *What examples of behavior, in a potential partner or myself, demonstrate these important qualities?*
5. *What relationships have I seen that illustrate James Crosby's A, H, and M?*

Skill: I understand the strengths and weaknesses in my family of origin and how those may affect me in my relationships.

Understand Your Family Background

Melanie and Kevin, newlyweds, were getting on each other's nerves. Melanie was irritated when Kevin asked her what she planned to buy every time she went shopping. Kevin didn't like it when Melanie asked him when he would be home every time he went out to see his friends. They finally figured out that they were hearing their parents' voices. Melanie heard her father warning her not to spend any more of his hard-earned money because "It doesn't grow on trees, you know." And Kevin heard his mother reminding him of the family curfew.

It wasn't hard for Melanie and Kevin to make some adjustments once they realized that the families they grew up in were still very much with them in the new family they were starting. It isn't always so easy.

Obviously, none of us is completely determined by our family of origin. But in our highly individualistic society, we often *overemphasize* the individual origins of our attitudes and *underemphasize* how much these ideas are influenced by how we were raised.

I usually ask engaged couples a few important questions about their families of origin: How many brothers and sisters do you have? How would you characterize your parents' relationship? Who in your family of origin are you most like and closest to? What about your extended family and those marriages? What is the most admirable marriage you've ever seen and why?

The answers to these questions often contain the keys that couples need to unlock the doors to their relationship. They discover that we are not really individuals. Rather, we are each a network of relationships.

Try this simple exercise. Write your name on a piece of paper, and draw an arrow pointing inward toward your name for every person you can think of who has influenced you as you became the person you are today. This will, no doubt, include parents and siblings, perhaps grandparents, teachers, pastors, friends. Without any one of these people in your life, you would be a different person in many ways. To take the exercise a step further, add a point to the other end of the arrows, and consider how you, in turn, have influenced the lives of these people. Without you, these people would be different persons today.

In the much-loved holiday classic movie *It's a Wonderful Life,* Clarence is an angel trying to get his wings. George Bailey is a young man caught in the midst of despair, wishing he had never been born. After George has an opportunity to see, in a virtual-reality experience, what life would have been like in his small town if he had never been born, Clarence comments, "Strange, isn't it? Each man's life touches so many other lives. And when he isn't around, he leaves an awful hole, doesn't he?" How true! Our lives form a marvelous network with others.

Within that network of relationships, each of us experiences the basic realities of life: trust, joy, love, hope, forgiveness, and pain. The seeds for our full humanity lie in those imperfect relationships; it is there, or not at all, that we gain the framework on which we can hang our language of faith when we say that God loves us with an everlasting love. As the Catholic tradition reminds us, with its focus on community, we do not come to God alone. That community even extends beyond time and space in the communion of saints, those men and women through the centuries who have influenced us as individuals and communities today. Community, in its various forms, shapes us; each of us is actually a *we* rather than an *I*, a dimension that we can often lose sight of today with our culture's intense focus on the individual. The first community we know is our family of origin.

What does all this have to do with marriage? Consider the following couples. A superficial glance at their families of origin suggests that they will face major adjustments in marriage. Julia grew up in a boisterous, Italian family, while

John had only one brother, and his family was quiet and private. Heidi was the oldest of three girls in her family, while Luis was the youngest of eight children. Shelly grew up in a farm family that worked the farm together, while Jay grew up in the city and lived with his mother after his parents divorced when he was fourteen.

Ethnicity, family size, birth order, geographic location, and issues of addictions, abuse, divorce, or disabilities — as well as many other variables in our family of origin — do make a difference in how we see the world. These influences show up in our interactions with a future spouse when it comes to issues of communication, roles, parenting, sexuality, religion, finances — any topic we tackle together. Often our behavior will be similar to what was modeled for us in our family of origin. Just as often, however, we will respond in ways completely different from what we were familiar with as children and adolescents. Either way, our family plays a large role in how we develop key values.

A clue to how connected an issue is to our family of origin may be our lack of willingness to discuss it or to consider options. Such a reluctance can be a friendly signal telling us that something about a particular topic — maybe not the topic in general, but a certain aspect of it — needs a serious look. This can be a painful exercise because some issues and our ways of dealing with them have just been that way without question. When two people consider marriage, they risk a great deal of hardship if they fail to take the time and risks

UNDERSTAND YOUR FAMILY BACKGROUND

involved in looking at some of these neglected areas. These areas need to be understood, and perhaps even negotiated, so that change can occur.

In many ways, our family of origin is a form of marriage preparation. I usually ask couples about the most admirable marriage they have seen, because what each person has seen of marriage in his or her life has helped form an idea of what marriage and intimacy can look like. In this sense, our marriage preparation has been going on, in our family of origin, in our extended families, in our faith communities, all our lives. Marriage preparation programs (see the appendix) might be considered *immediate* marriage preparation, following the *remote* preparation that's been happening for years.

Family as a System

Just remembering how things were, however, does not give us a full understanding of how and why our family of origin influences our intimate relationships. We need to understand how families operate in general. Indeed, each family is divinely and beautifully unique, but certain general dynamics are true of any family. We are beginning to understand more how families operate as a system, a system that goes through a complex cycle of stages in the course of its existence. When we understand that system, we better understand ourselves. And when we better understand ourselves, we are better equipped for the commitment of marriage.

First, what is a system? A system is simply a way of thinking about or looking at something. Unlike a mechanical or linear way of thinking, which organizes the pieces of a whole into steps or building blocks that follow one after the other, a system organizes the whole by all the pieces and how they interact. The best model for a system is probably a mobile, suspended from the ceiling and moving with every shift of the air around it. Every piece of the mobile is delicately connected to other pieces around it, and the whole is influenced by its surroundings. This is how a systems approach to thinking about family works. Instead of taking each part separately and focusing on it, a systems approach looks at the relationships and the processes at work in the system as a whole.

Family systems theory, the study of how families operate as a system and how that impacts family dynamics, is far more complex than we can explore here. However, a few basic facts about families, using the systems theory, will help us appreciate the influential nature of our family of origin.

- *A family system is more than the sum of its parts.* "The family" does not equal father + mother + daughter + son (or whoever the family members are). Rather, an energy is formed within this group when all or some of these people are present — an energy that is more than each individual separately. This is often referred to as synergy.

- *Every family has a set of rules.* Even though these rules are often unspoken, we can occasionally hear them articulated when someone insists, "But we always . . ." These implicit, unwritten rules have a great deal of power. Newlyweds can discover this quickly, for example, when it comes to Christmas traditions or how birthdays are celebrated — perhaps *even if* they're celebrated.

- *Families resist change.* Consider again the mobile. Imagine blowing on the mobile to make it sway. As soon as you cease to blow, the mobile will slowly try to reestablish homeostasis, a fancy word for a place of balance and rest. So, when Joe goes off to school (whether kindergarten or college) or Angie announces that she's engaged to be married, the family has a hard time adjusting to the change — even when it's a positive one. Each person has to change how he or she relates to this part of the system.

A student explained his family system in a paper for my class:

> The mobile that you used to demonstrate how situations in one family member's life can shake the whole family was very effective in helping me visualize the concept [of a web of relationships in a family]. I was reminded of a couple of years ago when my oldest brother had gotten his girlfriend pregnant and his fight for the custody of the child. This situation rocked our whole family, from grandparents to siblings, just as if we were really hanging on a mobile. At the time

67

I was wondering what would happen to all of the family, what effects the shaking would have on them. The place where the most important action took place, however, was not in the shaking family members like I would have expected. The most crucial action was in the pieces of string that held us together. For some members, the knots holding them to the rest of the mobile were loosened by all of the shaking, making them that much more likely to fall away from the family. But for the rest of the family, the shaking only pulled the knots tighter, making the family ties that much stronger and more secure. Blessed be the ties that bind.

The Family Life Cycle

The one constant in any family system is change: predictable shifts and stages that a family goes through. In our contemporary Western society, this family life cycle begins with a single young adult. Let's look at how these stages unfold and overlap into other stages.

The young adult. The period of time between leaving one's family home, marrying, and beginning one's own family is longer than has been the case in recent generations. During this in-between time, the young adult clarifies his or her values and personality and finishes the process of separating from the family of origin.

The newly married couple. The next stage involves newly-weds, who have many tasks to achieve together beyond their own intimacy and existence as a separate family unit. They work on issues of individual and couple identity, such as time with friends, times of solitude, and individual and joint interests. They also are faced with sorting out roles, careers, finances, sexuality, family planning, religion, and spirituality. Many couples describe the first year of marriage as hard or exhausting as well as good, precisely because there are so many issues to be worked out and clarified between them.

The new parents. The stage of early parenthood brings fresh challenges. The new parents now work to juggle their roles as parents in addition to what they already handle. Part of this process involves decisions about how to establish a healthy balance as spouses and parents in the midst of many other demands. Couples also need to learn how to relate to their parents as the grandparents of this new generation.

The school-age family. As each child begins to relate to a world beyond the family, to explore friendships and new skills, and to take on more responsibility within the household, the entire family undergoes a major shift. One significant challenge during this stage is the building of strong communication and conflict-resolution skills — skills that will play a significant role in the next stage.

The adolescent family. The family with adolescents balances the needs and values of the family with the increasing demands and attractions of the adolescent's peer group. Each

69

teen establishes his or her own identity and sense of self, while the parents deal with midlife issues and perhaps aging parents.

The launching family. This family focuses on directing and supporting their young adults in the challenge of building their own independent lives. Not only does this involve a regrouping of the remaining family members and of the couple, but the process may happen more than once. It isn't unusual, for example, for a young adult to attempt independence only to find that he or she needs to return home temporarily. At times, this stage may involve meshing with another family — such as in-laws if there is a marriage. This family also deals with the dying of the older generation.

The aging family. This family deals with retirement and coming to terms with physical limitations. At times, this may include being dependent on others. Family relationships primarily consist of relationships with adult children and grandchildren — and perhaps great-grandchildren. This family also deals with the death of a spouse as well as that of friends.

Bear in mind that this is a mere outline of predictable stages in a family life cycle and that each family goes through this cycle in its own unique way. Circumstances like cohabitation, divorce and possible remarriage, or teen pregnancy, for example, make this process much more complex than described here. What's more, most families find themselves in more than one stage at a time. School-age families may also have an adolescent, and the adolescent family may also be engaged in the challenges of the launching family.

While the youngest generation is coming to birth and experiencing childhood, the second generation is dealing with courtship and marriage, childbearing, and settling down. The third generation is dealing with being grandparents, entering a retirement lifestyle, and accepting the challenges and satisfactions of late adulthood.

In each stage (except, of course, the single young adult), the husband and wife have significant and unique challenges to face, which means they will need to call on the strengths of their relationship. Meanwhile, a couple's extended family and friends may be at very different stages in the family life cycle, dealing with a combination of other issues. Melanie and George, for example, ended up finding much of their support for dealing with their newborn twins from other parents of young children, because their parents were dealing with retirement and their siblings all had older children.

It helps to know how the families we grew up in shape us and influence our marriages. But it doesn't do much good unless we know how to talk about these issues and the myriad other matters that make up a shared life. That brings us to the next tool in our kit — a tool as indispensable as a hammer on a carpenter's belt.

It's time to talk about communication.

For Reflection

1. *What words would I use to describe my family of origin? Who am I closest to in my family of origin and why? What words would I use to describe my parents' marriage? What is the most admirable marriage I've ever seen and why?*

2. *How has my family of origin influenced me in my opinions about critical issues such as communication, intimacy, roles, finances, and sexuality?*

3. *What are the explicit (spoken) rules in my family system? What are the implicit (unspoken) rules in my family system?*

4. *When did my family system try to resist a change?*

5. *What families do I know in each of the stages of the family life cycle?*

UNDERSTAND YOUR FAMILY BACKGROUND

Skill: I communicate and listen effectively, and I am aware of the dynamics of the communication process.

Communicate
Effectively

Janeen and Mike used to communicate well. Now something is wrong. Janeen is feeling a lot of pressure at work. When she talks about it, she feels that Mike's response is to give her a lot of irrelevant advice. He's not really listening to her. Mike thinks that he's listening just fine and that his advice is pretty good. He doesn't understand what Janeen's problem is. He's afraid that she thinks something is wrong with him, so he often withdraws from these conversations. He nods and smiles and looks for ways to change the subject. That makes Janeen angry. That makes Mike angry.

Communication is the lifeblood of a relationship. Like many couples, Janeen and Mike need a transfusion.

I often draw a mobile on the blackboard when I talk to engaged couples about practical issues within marriage. I label the different parts of the mobile with the things the couples mention — time as a couple, time as a family, time as an individual, money, household chores, jobs. I then ask them what they would call the string from which the mobile is suspended — the one single connection that keeps the whole thing in balance. Someone will usually call out, "Communication!" How true — and how critical! Good communication is key to the process that is marriage.

Good communication is the *how* for most of the *what* that is discussed in this book and between any couple. Simply put, good communication is love in action. It draws on our nature as made in the image of God and thus motivates us to talk and listen within the framework of *love*. It assumes the best from the other person, and it offers respect, honesty, integrity, and generosity in every exchange. When I asked my students for a definition of love, a student with speech and physical disabilities suggested that love is learning another person's language. An insightful definition indeed and an excellent summary of good communication.

We will explore six keys to learning the other's language and the importance of that language within the context of marriage.

Listen well. When we think of communication, we often think of saying something effectively and clearly to be sure our point is not misunderstood. Communication theorists tell us, however, that 80 to 90 percent of good communication is listening, which is much more than hearing — and isn't easy.

Why is listening difficult? Listening is difficult because *it's not about me.* When I listen to the other, I set aside my own thoughts, feelings, and experiences to be fully present and attentive to what the other person is trying to say. To be present — the work of attention, as M. Scott Peck calls it in *The Road Less Traveled* — is hard work. Peck tells of listening to an hour-and-a-half lecture during which he was perspiring and after which he was exhausted because he had been paying such close attention to the speaker. Meanwhile, others left the same lecture disappointed because they didn't feel like they'd gotten much new information.

Being present goes beyond listening for new information. It involves the investment of my entire person in the process of being mindful of the other. I do not focus on myself, for example, by mentally comparing my past experience with what the other is saying. I do not filter the content and only listen for what's important to me. I do not judge the other and thus close myself off to the other's personhood and the importance of what is being communicated. I do not advise the other, thus ignoring his or her deepest concerns and feelings while rushing in with what I consider my own wisdom. I do not engage in mind reading, that is, predicting what the other is going to say and then not listening to what is actually being said. Most of all, I do not rehearse some mental script I am frantically drafting in response to what the other says. (I call this "listening with your motor running.")

Not feeling listened to is a lonely experience. One of my favorite cartoon strips, "Peanuts," captures this with sad humor. Charlie Brown is saying to Lucy, "I wish I could be happy. . . . I think I could be happy if my life had more purpose to it. . . . I also think that if I were happy, I could help others to be happy. . . . Does that make sense to you?" With the same facial expression she's had throughout the strip, Lucy responds, "We've had spaghetti at our house three times this month!" To this Charlie Brown can only groan his usual, "Good grief!"

Real listening is truly an art. I am aware of content; I hear facts; I watch for emotional expressions. At times, I may need to use the specific skill of active listening where, before responding, I paraphrase what I heard so that I don't proceed to respond to something that wasn't actually communicated. Paraphrasing begins something like this: "Let me see if I have this straight. You think that we should go to my parents' for Thanksgiving because it will be better weather than at Christmas, when it will be hard to travel. But at the same time, you're rather concerned about how welcome we really are at my parents' house. Is that right?" With that clarification, a direct and relevant response can be offered to which the other, in similar fashion, offers a paraphrase: "I hear you saying that your parents would be glad to have us, but the guest room is small and they worry about our being comfortable. Is that right?" Although a bit cumbersome and somewhat

COMMUNICATE EFFECTIVELY

slow, this approach can save a lot of energy when it comes to complex and highly sensitive issues.

Be honest, open, and accurate. This has to do with content. Being honest involves a measure of risk as I offer you my ideas and thoughts with appropriate and accurate details. Being open also involves risk, as I go beyond ideas and thoughts to share my feelings and opinions.

Accuracy is the dedicated effort I bring to being honest and open. When I am specific about what I like or find difficult, what I'm thinking or feeling, the other person receives the full breadth of what I'm trying to communicate. Expressing myself accurately means I avoid the tendency to use generalizations to enhance my point. Words like *always, never, everybody,* and *nobody* don't contribute to accuracy. Instead, they distract us with "how often" or "who"; they do not help us get to the issue. The clearer we are about what we're each thinking and feeling, the closer we come to the issues. Being accurate is the key.

In an article titled "Couples Should Fight for a Good Marriage" (*U.S. Catholic,* April 1994), Mary Lynn Hendrickson puts it strongly: "A marriage is a sham unless two people can be totally honest about what hurts and delights them."

Express yourself gently and with respect. This has to do with delivery. My words are gentle, not sarcastic, critical, or judgmental — especially of the other person. My tone of voice remains calm and moderate — without overtones of blame or criticism — which helps prevent the other from becoming defensive. It's worth a little extra time to weigh my words and to express myself gently and with respect because my words, once spoken, can never be retrieved or erased.

Recall that one of David Augsberger's inaccurate notions of love noted in the chapter "Skill Two: Let Others Get Close" (page 35) was "Love is understanding: If you love me you will know what I need or want without my telling or asking." The ability to read the other person's mind doesn't come with the relationship or even with the marriage license; I need to say what I need—gently and with respect.

Use I-messages. An *I*-message tells you how *I* feel, not how *you* made me feel. You cannot make me feel anything; I choose to feel the way I feel. One form of the *I*-message is called the *XYZ* statement, which gives the other person specific information about the circumstance and how I feel. "When you do *X* in situation *Y*, I feel *Z*." For example, I might tell a child, "When you throw a tantrum in the grocery store when you want something I won't buy, I feel angry because I am embarrassed by how you are acting." Or I might tell a spouse, "When you leave your dirty coffee cup on the counter rather than putting it in the dishwasher, I feel frustrated." Each of these situations gives the other person specific information about the circumstances and how I am feeling. It allows the other to respond without being defensive. A special note of caution: Do not, as I already mentioned, use generalizations. "You always leave your dirty coffee cup on the counter rather than putting it in the dishwasher, and I feel

COMMUNICATE EFFECTIVELY

frustrated" is not an authentic *I*-message.

Be aware of nonverbal messages. Whether I'm speaking or listening, nonverbal messages are as important as verbal expressions. Whether it's eye contact, posture, or facial expression, I say volumes without a single word. For example, if I'm standing above a seated adult or a small child, a conversation between equals is very difficult. In that position, there's a built-in sense of power or strength that can easily intimidate and thus inhibit good communication. Most people would agree that if there's a discrepancy between the verbal information and the nonverbal messages, the nonverbal messages are probably the more reliable. If a friend tells me that he or she is fine, but the tone of voice, facial expression, or other clues tell me otherwise, I may want to check further.

Avoid gunnysacking. Gunnysacking is the practice of avoiding conflict by stuffing the issue out of the way because "It's just a little thing." This is a common human tendency — with long-range damaging effects. If something really annoys me, I can ignore it, hoping it might just vanish into thin air. But I'm not really ignoring it; I'm tucking it away in my gunnysack, along with other issues that have bugged me but that I haven't bothered to bring up. Eventually and inevitably, the gunnysack reaches its limit and bursts, with an avalanche of complaints, accusations, and threats. Usually, the other person doesn't know what just hit. Dealing with the issues as they come along, even acknowledging, "I know this is a little problem, but it bothers me," can help prevent gunnysacking and minimize the chances of issues mounting up.

These six keys to learning the other's language — listening well; being honest, open, and accurate; expressing yourself gently and with respect; using *I*-messages; being aware of nonverbal messages; and avoiding gunnysacking — can be applied to any relationship: family relationships, relationships in the workplace or faith community, as well as friendships. The skills are the same; the content is different.

When applied to the intimate relationship of a couple, especially in marriage, these keys are especially critical because both partners have much more at risk. They have committed their lives to the mutual good of each other and the growth-filled journey of a sacramental life. Good communication is the way their commitment is going to endure — even thrive.

Communication Style as a Couple

We each have an individual style of communication that begins to evolve in early childhood as we become familiar with language, structure, and delivery. Our natural temperament and our surroundings contribute to the communication style that comes to be natural to us. How quickly or slowly we talk, whether we use our hands when we talk, whether we add minute details to our content, and other expressions and mannerisms are part of our individual communication style.

Family history and ethnic background can play a big role in our communication patterns and expectations. If you come from a family of yellers — except you prefer to say that your family simply communicated at the top of their voices — and I come from a family where we didn't talk about disagreements or anything controversial, we may be in for an interesting time of it.

We bring our individual communication styles together and gradually form a style as a couple. Who talks more? Who introduces a topic for discussion? Do we interrupt each other much? How do we handle disagreements? Does the disagreement get resolved — or just dropped? Are there topics we never risk discussing? The good news is, we can modify bad communication habits by being intentional about our communication patterns as a couple before they get too established.

After twenty years of work, Dr. John Gottman and a team of researchers at the University of Washington can now predict, with more than 90 percent accuracy, those couples who will have a lasting marriage and those who won't. They base their assessment on key dynamics in communication by gathering data as couples interact. They study two partners by videotaping their exchanges and by measuring their pulse. With this information, the researchers gain insights about communication styles and emotions exhibited by the couple in various exchanges. They also follow up with these couples years later to see how their marriages are doing.

Surprisingly, Gottman has found that anger and fighting are not the greatest problems couples deal with. Rather, he refers to the "four horsemen of the Apocalypse" as the real problems: criticism, contempt, defensiveness, and withdrawal.

Criticism. Gottman identifies criticism as attacking the personhood of another. "You are stupid" and "You are lazy" are criticisms; they are statements that directly attack the other person's selfhood and disregard the person's innate goodness. Comments that focus on the person's specific behavior prove to be much less damaging to the exchange. Talking about the problems involved in bouncing a check is much more productive than calling the other person stupid. Discussing the feelings of frustrations about leaving dirty clothes on the bedroom floor leads to understanding quicker than calling the other person lazy. Criticism usually involves generalizing, blaming, or accusing, and it engenders criticism in return. As a result, neither person feels like the relationship is a safe place to bring emotions.

Contempt. Gottman sees insult and psychological abuse as being at the heart of contempt — which, he says, should be outlawed in marriage. Sarcasm, mocking, and name-calling are forms of verbal abuse used to tear down the other's character, creating a thick layer of animosity. Contempt can be expressed nonverbally as well as verbally, such as a look of scorn that a roll of the eyes can convey. Contempt rips at the fabric of a relationship and leads both partners to lose sight of the positive qualities in each other that drew them together in the first place.

Defensiveness. According to Gottman, defensiveness consists of denying responsibility, making excuses, whining, and throwing counterattacks. Defensiveness further poisons the already negative environment and tends to escalate the conflict rather than resolve it.

Withdrawal. When the conflict gets too hot and one person "checks out," true communication is no longer possible. According to Gottman, withdrawal is the mental, emotional, or physical unavailability of a person. When a person habitually and/or intentionally shuts down and withdraws, he or she conveys disapproval, distance, and smugness.

When any or all of these "four horsemen" are regularly present in a couple's communication, there is cause for concern. Gottman emphasizes the importance of affirmation in healthy couple communication. He suggests a ratio of five positive, affirming comments to one comment that is negative or complaining. Sadly, the atmosphere created by criticism, contempt, defensiveness, and withdrawal leaves one little motivated to even focus on the good of the other, let alone comment on it.

One other aspect of Gottman's research is worth noting. His work has identified three kinds of successfully married couples, who vary significantly in how they handle disagreements: *validating couples, volatile couples,* and *conflict-avoiding couples.* Validating couples tend to listen well to each other and work out their differences without a lot of scream-ing. Volatile couples thrive on emotional intensity and may fight bitterly, but they make up with the same amount of emotional intensity and have a great deal of passion in their marriage. Conflict-avoiding couples have a restrained style that may seem unhealthy and unemotional from the outside. The lack of intensity, however, is comfortable for them.

All three kinds of couples can achieve a lasting marriage, Gottman's researchers conclude, as long as the five-to-one ratio of constructive to destructive comments is maintained.

Little Things Make a Big Difference

There's an old song about little things meaning a lot, which is especially true in marriage. In the daily routines of life, the little things — negative and positive — enhance or inhibit good communication. Marriages rarely die of a massive coro-nary. Rather, they slowly bleed to death from the little things that build up day by day, especially those little things that are not dealt with. Little things like how the toilet paper comes off the roll, how the toothpaste tube is squeezed, and whether the lights get turned off or not are the small and seemingly insignificant details that can smother a marriage and leave it nearly lifeless.

Little thoughtful things, however, like a note under the pillow, a call at work to see how the other's day is going, or an unexpected hug while sharing chores tells the other person

COMMUNICATE EFFECTIVELY

that he or she is not taken for granted. Such small gestures add up and keep the relationship vibrant and exciting.

One of the positive little things that strengthens a marriage and encourages good communication day in and day out is the humble and genuine willingness to say, "I'm sorry." Recall the 1970 movie *Love Story*, which featured the saying "Love means never having to say you're sorry." The fact is, love *does* mean having to say, "I'm sorry" — over and over again, sometimes for the same thoughtless or insensitive behavior. Day by day, husband and wife build a grace-filled rhythm of forgiveness and reconciliation when they can say, "I'm sorry" and generously accept simple apologies.

Jennie and Jeff, for example, always know when the other is ready to make up. The little heart-shaped pillow that Jennie's aunt gave them for a wedding present gets tossed on the bed as a signal that the person is ready to apologize and make up.

So if the little things can be so significant, what would be your nomination for the most deadly enemy to good communication as a couple? Mine would be boredom. As routine inevitably sets in, it's easy for my husband and me to settle into "What was in the mail?" and "Anything new around here?" and forget to really talk with each other about what we're thinking and feeling on a deeper-than-daily level.

One way couples keep boredom at bay is to go out regularly on dates. I am proud to say that nary a week has gone by in the past twenty-five years that my husband, Mitch, and I have not gone out for an evening to just enjoy each other — usually taking in a movie or play. We figure we could have redone the whole interior of our house with the money we've spent through the years, but maybe we wouldn't know or enjoy each other as much. Intentional efforts to avoid boredom take energy, time, and mutual respect. The end result, however, is a relationship that is always new, interesting, and surprising.

Another deadly enemy to a marriage may be as difficult to notice as boredom: the constant noise around us. We live in a fast-paced world, full of noisy machines, expectations, and demands, and — unfortunately — our bodies don't come equipped with "earlids." Unlike our eyes, which have those thin but powerful lids that let us shut out harsh, piercing, and distracting light, our ears get hit with the daily noise of life around us. Taken little by little, the noise may seem hardly noticeable; collectively, however, it can create a powerful din. In the process of tuning out the noise around us in order to stay healthy, it is easy to tune out each other as well.

Every couple who works on communication will learn that men and women speak and listen differently. This is but one aspect of the next skill we will consider — coming to terms with the profound differences between the sexes, and particularly differences in gender roles.

For Reflection

1. *Whom do I know who is an especially effective communicator? Why?*

2. *Whom do I know who is an especially poor communicator? Why?*

3. *In a particular situation, how can I tell if I'm gunnysacking? How can I tell when I'm nagging? How can I tell when something needs to be addressed?*

4. *Which of the keys to good communication do I need to work on? Why?*

5. *How often do I say, "I'm sorry" to those who are important to me?*

Skill: *I am aware of gender and role issues in contemporary culture and how they can affect a marriage, and I am able to communicate about them.*

Examine
Gender Roles

Before they got married, Crystal and Tyson agreed that they would not divide chores according to gender. When something needed to be done around the house, whoever saw the need would take care of it. However, since the birth of their daughter, life has gotten more complicated, and Crystal and Tyson are getting confused about roles. Tyson thinks that Crystal does more than he expects. Crystal feels like she is doing all the mothering. Should she? Does Tyson expect her to? They've tried to talk about this but haven't gotten very far.

It was simpler for Crystal and Tyson's parents and grand-parents. A generation ago, women and men seemed to know what their roles were and what was expected of them. Take a look at this excerpt from a 1950s home-economics textbook titled *How to Be a Good Wife*:

Have dinner ready. Plan ahead, even the night before, to have a delicious meal — on time. This is a way of letting him know that you have been thinking about him and are concerned about his needs. Most men are hungry when they come home and the prospect of a good meal is part of the warm welcome needed.

Prepare yourself. Take 15 minutes to rest so that you'll be refreshed when he arrives. Touch up your makeup, put a ribbon in your hair and be fresh-looking. He has just been with a lot of work-weary people. . . .

Prepare the children: Take a few minutes to wash the children's hands and faces (if they are small), comb their hair, and if necessary, change their clothes. . . .

Listen to him: You may have a dozen things to tell him, but the moment of his arrival is not the time. Let him talk first. . . .

The goal: Try to make your home a place of peace and order where your husband can renew himself in body and spirit.

While the reality was not this simple, of course, the expectations were. The code of conduct was clear about what men and women were to do and say. Today, the expectations are unclear, and there isn't really a code of conduct. For example, is it polite for a man to hold the door open for a woman, or in doing so, is he implying that she can't do it for herself? Do the husband's career ambitions and opportunities take precedence over the wife's, or do the ambitions and opportunities of both get serious consideration? If a child is sick, does the mother rearrange her day — perhaps missing work — so that child can see a doctor, or is there some discussion between the parents about the best way to handle the situation?

These questions are directly related to gender and roles. *Gender* refers to those qualities and behaviors associated with being masculine or feminine in a particular society. It doesn't take a degree in sociology to see that in our society today there is a wide variety of gender roles within marriage. One way to form today's questions about gender and roles is by looking closely at the advantages and disadvantages of the roles as they were traditionally understood.

I often do this with my students. I ask them to identify the characteristics associated with the past stereotypes of "real" men and women. The students usually come up with words and phrases like *rational, strong,* and *focused on tasks outside the home* for men, and *emotional, weak,* and *focused on tasks in the home* for women.

Then I ask them to name the advantages and disadvantages of the traditional roles they've just described. It's fairly easy for them to come up with disadvantages: a person's possibilities are limited, especially if his or her talents and interests don't happen to fit the stereotypes. The students find it difficult, however, to name the advantages of traditional roles, concluding that expectations are clearer and people know what is expected of them. I usually have to point out that traditional roles are clear about who handles child care, an issue that becomes complex when the stereotypes begin to shift.

Wouldn't it seem that we have moved beyond these stereotypes and limited expectations of one another? Yes, we are in that process, but the deeply rooted ways of thinking about roles are still very much with us today, perhaps more in some areas of the country than in others. When we've grown up with a secure understanding of what we could expect of our mothers and our fathers, it's hard to shift gears to other possibilities, even if we want to. But in a world where more and more women are focusing on careers, and men are more aware of their appearance and their nurturing tendencies, our ideas about what it means to be masculine or feminine are challenged.

Men and women considering the commitment of marriage need to be aware of how those old expectations are still at work and may cause tension and misunderstandings unless they are critically examined.

A Language of Our Own

Sociolinguist Dr. Deborah Tannen helps us understand how gender differences influence our communication. Her research indicates that women and men, at times, speak a different "language." In her book *You Just Don't Understand,* she explains that these differences go back to childhood socialization and the fact that girls and boys tend to play and grow up differently. She suggests that most girls grow up having a best friend, and talking is one of the main activities they do together. Boys, on the other hand, play games in groups, with rules and winners and losers. As a result, she concludes, adult men and women communicate differently.

- Men focus on the content of a conversation (the *what*) while women focus on the process (the *how*).
- Men prefer side-by-side communication while women prefer face-to-face interactions.
- Men are geared toward independence while women are geared toward intimacy.
- Men listen to the content of what's being said before they indicate agreement, while women nod and give nonverbal assurance to let the speaker know, "I'm listening and engaged in what you're saying."
- Men look for solutions to problems while women look for ways to explore the problem thoroughly — a process Tannen calls "troubles talk."

Tannen doesn't conclude that one way is right and the other is wrong, rather that men and women have different ways of doing things and that this needs to be acknowledged and respected. When I share Dr. Tannen's research with

EXAMINE GENDER ROLES

students and couples in marriage enrichment sessions, the reaction is often one of recognition: "That's just what happens with us!" (Bear in mind the nature of generalities; inevitably, there are those individuals who are exceptions to these patterns.)

Where to Start with the New Questions

Women have always worked, of course, whether inside the home or out. Two-career families, however, are now the norm, which brings up questions that families didn't have to face on a regular basis in the past. For example, chores such as doing laundry, cleaning, and cooking — traditionally handled by women — need to be reviewed in light of the overall family situation. Otherwise, Mom ends up with a second shift after she comes home from an already busy day.

Career opportunities, especially those that involve relocation, need to be discussed alongside the career opportunities for a spouse. The equal responsibilities and privileges of maternity and paternity need to be acknowledged and respected in the family and the workplace, as does child care. Finding a safe and nurturing place to take children while parents are at work is never easy because no one can give a child what his or her parents can, and safe, quality care is hard to find. Questions of equal pay for men and women handling similar responsibilities in similar positions, regardless of who is head of the household, become issues of justice.

EXAMINE GENDER ROLES

These and many similar issues have yet to be adequately addressed as changes in our society force our old stereotypes into question.

The more women and men are able to see their respective possibilities as limitless, the more families and society as a whole will benefit, as the following essay by Nancy Smith reminds us:

> For every woman who is tired of acting weak when she is strong, there is a man who is tired of appearing strong when he feels vulnerable;
>
> For every woman who is tired of acting dumb, there is a man who is burdened with the constant expectation of knowing everything;
>
> For every woman who is tired of being called "an emotional female," there is a man who is denied the right to weep and to be gentle;
>
> For every woman who is called unfeminine when she competes, there is a man for whom competition is the only way to prove his masculinity;
>
> For every woman who is tired of being a sex object, there is a man who must worry about his potency;
>
> For every woman who feels "tied down" by her children, there is a man who is denied the full pleasure of parenthood;

EXAMINE GENDER ROLES

For every woman who is denied meaningful employment or equal pay, there is a man who was not taught the satisfaction for another human being;

For every woman who was not taught the intricacies of an automobile, there is a man who was not taught the satisfaction of cooking;

For every woman who takes a step toward her own liberation, there is a man who finds the way to freedom has been made a little easier.

Fortunately, many couples are stepping into these challenges with grace and comfort. They readily admit what they like and don't like to do, and they work out the issues from there. Some couples, for example, have turned the stereotypes completely around: he handles household chores and childcare responsibilities while she enters the workplace. There are people, of course, who have talked about roles and responsibilities and have concluded that, in fact, the traditional roles are the most comfortable and appropriate for them.

Whatever determinations are made regarding roles, the process is the same for every couple. We begin with an examination of how our family of origin assigned roles and what we liked and didn't like about how that worked. Next we ask ourselves what it means to *us* to be husband and wife and what our own unique talents and interests are.

As long as issues are discussed and choices are freely made — after looking at various options — the spouses'

EXAMINE GENDER ROLES

ultimate decision will be right for them at that point in time. As with any arrangement, however, details need periodic review. A couple's current understanding may shift significantly in the future, with any number of changes in life circumstances.

These can be extremely difficult issues for a husband and wife to work out. As they sort them out, they will learn more fully what *masculine* and *feminine* really mean. These differences show up with particular intensity in sexuality — our next skill.

For Reflection

1. *What other traditional and stereotypical qualities do I associate with gender?*
2. *What other advantages or disadvantages do I see to traditional gender roles?*
3. *How do I see today's toys reinforcing traditional male and female stereotypes? How do I see them breaking down traditional stereotypes?*
4. *What does "being a wife" mean to me? What does "being a husband" mean to me?*
5. *What differences have I noticed in the communication patterns of women and men?*

EXAMINE GENDER ROLES

Skill: *I am aware of and comfortable with my own sexuality, that of the opposite sex, and sexuality in general.*

Get Comfortable
with Sex

Ron and Susan are afraid sex is going to be a problem after they get married. Ron's upbringing causes him to think of sex with embarrassment. Susan was married before. Her marriage, which was annulled in the Catholic Church, involved sexual abuse. They look forward to having a fulfilling sexual relationship once they are married, but they are apprehensive about it and have difficulty talking about it. It's clear to both of them that they don't know very much about a healthy sexuality.

Ron and Susan have grown up in a society where sex and the human body have a high profile and are used to sell everything from toothpaste to tires. How does one cultivate a healthy and balanced attitude toward sexuality? How do Christian values come into play? How does sexuality take its proper place in a marriage without overwhelming the rest of the relationship or getting lost in the busyness of everyday life?

Most of us find ourselves somewhat ambivalent about our bodies and our sexuality. The Christian tradition, for reasons we will explore later in this chapter, has also shared in this ambivalence. But we only need to look again at chapter 1 of Genesis to get a fuller understanding of creation and the splendor of humankind: "Then God said, 'Let us make humankind in our image, according to our likeness. . . .' And it was so. God saw everything that he had made, and indeed, it was very good" (Genesis 1:26, 30 – 31). From the outset, the human body was good; it imaged, in some way, the essence of God. Yet generation after generation lost sight of that essential reality, leaving us today with mixed — and often confusing — attitudes about the human body and how it relates physically to its surrounding world.

Our Catholic faith has a long tradition of upholding the beauty and sanctity of the human body and the respect due our sexuality. Following the wisdom of many teachers throughout the church's history, the fathers of the Second Vatican Council issued *The Pastoral Constitution on the Church in the Modern World (Gaudium et Spes),* in which we read:

> Though made of body and soul, man is one. Through his bodily composition, he gathers to himself the elements of the material world. Thus they reach their

crown through him, and through him raise their voices in free praise of the Creator.

For this reason man is not allowed to despise his bodily life. Rather, he is obliged to regard his body as good and honorable since God has created it and will raise it up on the last day. (n. 14)

More recently, Pope John Paul II's letter *The Christian Family in the Modern World (Familiaris Consortio)* puts it this way:

Sexuality, by means of which man and woman give themselves to one another through the acts which are proper and exclusive to spouses, is not something simply biological, but concerns the innermost being of the human person as such. It is realized in a truly human way only if it is an integral part of the love by which a man and woman commit themselves totally to one another until death. (n. 11)

This relatively recent teaching on marriage represents an important development in the church's understanding of sexuality. Prior to the Second Vatican Council in the mid-1960s, the church often talked about children as the primary end of marriage, with the secondary purpose being the good of the couple. Since the Second Vatican Council, however, the church has consistently and officially taught that marriage is

GET COMFORTABLE WITH SEX

for the good of the couple's relationship as well as for the good of any children who may be born into the marriage.

This evolution of thought and teaching has resulted in serious theological reflections on the beauty of sexuality and how much it can teach us about the mystery of human relationships. In an article titled "The Pope, Genesis and Human Sexuality" (*America,* September 27, 1980), author Mary G. Durkin comments on Pope John Paul II's series of reflections on sexuality preceding an international synod on the family held in Rome in 1980. She quotes the pope as saying:

> We need to celebrate human sexuality because through it we discover the meaning of life. . . . Through physical nakedness we discover that man and woman are two different ways of being human and thus come to an understanding of the importance of unselfish giving of ourselves as we become "one" but remain two individuals. The love needed for truly unselfish giving is a model for all true human communication. When a man discovers the femininity of a woman and she the masculinity of him, they both arrive at a deeper appreciation of the meaning of their lives.

As we continue to reflect on, understand, and articulate what a holistic vision of the human person looks like, especially in terms of our sexuality, the Catholic tradition has much to offer, because its vision of sexuality comes from its view of marriage as a sacrament, explored further in the chapter "Skill Nine: Grow in the Spiritual Life" (page 131).

But how do we "celebrate human sexuality," as Pope John Paul II says? How do we venture into our inhibitions about sex to find lifelong and satisfying sexual expressions within the context of marriage? We begin with a clearer understanding of what sex is.

Some Facts of Life

Understanding our own sexuality is a lifelong process. That process evolves through the years and is best advanced with an appreciation for the basic facts of life. Let's consider some of those facts about the wonder of God's gift of human sexuality.

- *Sex is important to who we are.* For example, what's the first question anyone asks about a newborn infant? We want to know whether it's a boy or a girl. We don't know how to relate to human persons apart from that identity, an identity that is linked to their sexuality.

- *Every cell of the human body is either male or female in its chromosomes.* Our sexual identity is not limited to our genital areas but is a factor in all that we do, from talking to playing to praying. Our sexuality is far more than just genital sexual activity.

- *We are built for touch.* According to a wonderful book by anthropologist Ashley Montagu titled *Touching: The Human Significance of the Skin,* skin is the largest and most sensitive organ of the human body. It is how we receive most of our information. We long to know ourselves as cherished in simple skin-to-skin contact.

- *Human sexuality is meant for more than procreation.* What happens in the relationship between a man and a woman is creative of the two of them as well as potentially of a child. While a woman is always attractive to her mate and usually available for lovemaking, her fertility is occasional and not usually known to herself or others. Intercourse in humans is not strictly tied to times of fertility or being "in heat," like it is for many other species.

- *The context for lovemaking is essential.* The same objective act of sexual intercourse that can be a celebration of deep love and long-term commitment between a husband and wife can also be brutal rape in a very different situation. That context, then, makes all the difference in what the act means to the people involved.

What, then, do we do with these facts of life about human sexuality? Western culture seems to have had a particularly difficult time developing a balanced approach to this powerful human experience, with the pendulum swinging back and forth between permissive and restrictive approaches. Why?

Dualism and Sex

Many thinkers suggest that a dualistic approach to the human person has contributed to our culture's lack of appreciation for sex. The theory of dualism originated in the early centuries after Christ with the Neoplatonist philosophers (followers of Plato's thought), who considered the soul and the body as two distinct and conflicting parts of the human person. This thinking positioned the lower physical desires at war with the higher needs of the spirit. Since sexuality was part of the physical realm, it was seen as far less important than the soul, which was capable of love and things spiritual.

Dualism regarding the human person is not just a phenomenon of the past, however; it continues to plague our view of the human person. Whenever we consider one part of the human person apart from the full person, we are guilty of our own form of dualism. Hollywood and other media offer their own version of dualism; having sex, for example, is portrayed as just another form of recreation, totally independent of any deep intimacy or long-term commitment. Whether it's excessive dieting or exercising, preoccupation with appearance, or other behavior that focuses primary attention on the body to the neglect of the spirit — or vice versa — the result is pain for the entire person. We are a holistic reality, and we need to honor that. I don't so much *have* a body as I *am* a body.

Although dualism is not Christian in its origins — the Jewish culture out of which Jesus came was and is very respectful of the body — it has heavily influenced Christian thinking about the human person and sexuality. Early in her history, beginning with the centuries immediately following the death of Jesus, the church developed a dualistic approach to human sexuality, since that was the atmosphere in which her reflection was taking place. As a result, for much of the church's history, sex in marriage was merely tolerated and seen as valuable only for the good of having children.

The healthier and more holistic view and theology of the body and sexuality on the part of the Catholic Church since Vatican II is well exemplified in this section from *The Christian Family in the Modern World* (1981):

> Conjugal love involves a totality, in which all the elements of the person enter — appeal of the body and instinct, power of feeling and affectivity, aspiration of the spirit and of will. It aims at a deeply personal unity, a unity that, beyond unity in one flesh, leads to forming one heart and soul. (n. 13)

What are the elements of a healthy sexuality that lead to the couple's unity of heart and soul?

GET COMFORTABLE WITH SEX

The Elements of a Healthy Sexuality

Early in a marriage, sexual satisfaction usually comes comfortably, almost naturally. We enjoy playful exploration and delightful discoveries of own body and our beloved's. Time need not rob us of this satisfaction, and it won't — if we appreciate the elements of a healthy sexuality.

For example, couples need *proper knowledge and information.* This includes proper terminology. Believe it or not, this can be a problem for many people who, from toilet-training days, have been taught cute little names for the genitals, such as "pee-pee" and "woo-woo." Caught in their own inhibitions about the human body — their own and others — parents often have a hard time using words like *penis* and *vagina* as comfortably as they use words like *elbow* and *knee.* Instead, they find cute labels that cover their discomfort, leaving their children with a seriously bankrupt vocabulary for an essential part of their lives. By the time these children grow up and enter intimate relationships, they have probably dropped the childhood labels for the correct terminology, but the inhibitions "caught" in childhood seldom get dropped with the labels. How am I to be comfortable and honest in telling you what's going on with my body and my sexuality if I can't even use the proper terminology?

Couples also need thorough and accurate information about how reproduction happens and the basic physiology involved. Despite the basic facts they memorized in high

GET COMFORTABLE WITH SEX

school biology classes, couples are often surprised at how helpful a review of the basics of human reproduction can be. There are a number of reliable books available that present this information in straightforward and respectable terms. (See suggested reading.)

This information should include a careful review of the complexity of female sexuality or — as my husband, Mitch, so colorfully describes it — the differences between "indoor plumbing and outdoor plumbing." In addition to arousal and intercourse that is also a part of his sexuality, for example, she has three other aspects at work in her sexuality. She experiences the monthly cycle of menstruation, the process of pregnancy, and the effects of breast-feeding (if she chooses) as part of her sexuality. Because these aspects affect her sexuality, the sexuality of the couple is affected as well. Both partners need to be aware of and appreciate the complexity of the way her body is created.

In addition to basic information about reproduction and the complexities of female sexuality, both husband and wife need to appreciate how much they can teach each other about their own unique sexuality, thus enhancing the sexuality they share together. After all, our sexuality is as unique as the rest of our personhood. We cannot read sex manuals or talk with professionals to find out about our deepest sexual selves. Only spouses can know this much detail about their bodies. Only in the trust-filled intimacy of their relationship,

GET COMFORTABLE WITH SEX

where such discussions are safe, can this kind of information —
these kinds of discoveries — be shared.

Another element of healthy sexuality is a sound understanding of and appreciation for sexuality as an *energy toward
intimacy,* a powerful energy that draws us toward each other.
This is the energy that urges each of us beyond our usual safety
zone to share ourselves and risk yet more intimacy with each
other. This energy, of course, can be misused and abused, just
as other aspects of the human person can be.

Understanding sexuality as a *powerful language* is another
element of healthy sexuality. This splendid language can teach
a husband and wife much about their relationship as well
as help them express what they mean to each other. In their
lovemaking, the two say much about their relationship: from
being naked with each other, physically as well as emotionally, to being together and being apart, to entering and being
entered, to experiencing pleasure in giving the other pleasure.
This language of intimate love goes beyond what words
capture.

At the center of this powerful language of sexuality is
the experience of touch. Each of our lives began in touch and
lovemaking, and more life continues to happen, at its best,
when we touch each other. If we don't continue to be touched,
held, and hugged, something within us withers in every part
of who we are. In the fusion of hearts and bodies, each of us
came to be; we are products of intimacy — sexual, physical,
full intimacy — and we long for that for ourselves. That

longing for intimacy and the desire to be in a relationship is deeply mysterious and deeply at the heart of who we are. It is both deeply physical and deeply spiritual. In making love with another, I am saying, "This is my body, my whole self given for you. In the love that we are expressing we touch God's love for each of us and celebrate that love in a way that generates more love." Hence our term *making love.*

A final element of healthy sexuality is an awareness of sexuality as an *integral part of the relationship.* Couples need to make love all day long if, at the end of their busy days, they are to come together in physical, sexual, and mutually satisfying ways. If there are problems with a couple's sexuality, for example, most likely there are problems in the rest of the relationship as well. That's why a marriage counselor or sex therapist, meeting with spouses who have concerns about their sex life, will often ask about finances, children and extended-family relationships, day-to-day stress, and other issues. The professional will not narrow the focus to sex but will ask both partners to look at the full picture of their life, of which their sexuality is an integral part. (Occasionally, of course, the problem is a physical dysfunction. But most of the time, the sexual relationship is a good barometer of what is or isn't happening in the rest of the relationship.)

What about Premarital Sex?

Because sexuality is such an important part of a couple's whole relationship, being sexually intimate before marriage is an important topic. Premarital sex is also more common than it has been in the past.

Figures from the U.S. Census Bureau indicate that in 1990 there were 2.9 million unmarried couples living together, up 80 percent from 1980, and this trend shows no signs of lessening.

Among the many factors contributing to the rise in cohabitation are the pressures from media, a broader social acceptance of such arrangements, and the availability of more reliable birth-control methods. In addition, there seems to be a tension between earlier physical maturity today and a later age at which marriage is feasible because of economic or educational needs. In other words, people are physically ready for marriage at earlier ages, but at the same time, they're not ready by a different set of standards. This leaves a much longer time of potential sexual frustration for teens and young adults than was the case in the past.

Another factor contributing to a greater frequency of premarital sex may be what we call "skin hunger," the longing that each of us has for a certain amount of touch and physical closeness — a longing that is not satisfied by a culture that is increasingly impersonal and individualistic and doesn't touch. Holding hands, giving a quick kiss, or patting someone on the back — these holy and gentle touches have become risky, fed by fear of accusations regarding harassment or objectification. One way some people may attempt to meet their needs for being held is through premarital sex. As a single woman put it, "There are days when I would come home alone to my apartment at the end of the day, just aching to be held."

My husband and I have developed a three-part theory that explains why our culture is plagued with misunderstandings about nakedness, sex, and intimacy; we call it our theory of instant intimacy. We start with the fact that human intimacy is both the most desired human experience and the most risky one, which usually — although not always — takes time to establish. (Remember "taming" in *The Little Prince* in the chapter "Skill Two: Let Others Get Close"?) We add to that fact our culture's "instant mentality"; most of us have little patience for anything that takes time — from gourmet food to weight loss. As a result, we try to "instantize" this very desirable intimacy by engaging in the physically intimate action of sex, without establishing genuine emotional intimacy. Too often, the results are deeply wounding. Instead of finding a shortcut to intimacy, the process actually short-circuits itself, as we're left feeling empty and lost.

Is instant intimacy a problem? In his recent book titled *Marriage Savers: Helping Your Friends and Family Stay Married,* Michael J. McManus cites recent studies of couples who live together. According to McManus, these studies indicate that couples who cohabit before marriage have a higher divorce rate — 50 to 100 percent higher — than those couples who do not. The paradox is, many people who cohabit do so in order to help insure marital compatibility, based on the fear of repeating the marital failures they see around them. The problem is, living together doesn't necessarily prove we can be married well; it only tells us whether or not we can live together!

Columnist Art A. Bennett, in an article titled "Why Co-habiting Is a Bad Idea" *(Catholic Faith and Family,* December 13 – 19, 1998) points out the consumerist mentality of co-habitation: "Cohabiting couples, in fact, are treating each other like an object that needs to be tested for flaws. They behave as if they want to test-drive their relationships to see how they handle around the curves, to walk around in the new shoes to see if they cause blisters." He goes on to say, "Cohabiting means opting for a consumerist yardstick that is entirely inappropriate in a spiritual, moral, and emotional context such as marriage. A couple can't test each other out in this fashion because the test is missing two critical ingre-dients: commitment and grace."

In an article titled "The Cohabitation Trap" *(Cosmopolitan,* March 1994), Laura Schlessinger, known on the radio and in newspapers as Dr. Laura, invites her readers to stand in the woman's shoes. She offers this characteristically blunt advice: "Moving in with a man when you don't know how he feels is to try to make him feel something toward you. That's demeaning and stupid. It is about you auditioning." Later she gives her underlying reason: "My concern is that when relationships prematurely take on elements of sexuality and living-in, it makes it more difficult to have the objectivity required to make a good decision."

Despite current cultural trends and pressures, it's refreshing to find these various counsels that, in effect, support the Catholic Church's teaching regarding sexual intimacy. In his booklet titled *Living Together and the Christian Commitment*, author James Healy summarizes the church's teaching: "We in the Catholic Church believe that sexual intimacy finds its true home in marriage, a public, faithful, exclusive commitment to each other and an equally important lifelong commitment to the children who may be created from this marriage."

Author Christine Gudorf supports the church's teaching on premarital sex and emphasizes its sacred dimension. In her excellent article titled "Why Sex Is So Good for Your Marriage" *(U.S. Catholic,* November 1992), she goes right to the height of pleasure in sex and finds a divine parallel: "For many persons the experience of orgasm in loving marriage is the clearest experience of the divine they have ever known. In this orgasmic experience we feel known to the depth of our souls, loved by one from whom we have no secrets, and freed to risk ourselves, let go of our very consciousness, and become totally vulnerable to the loved one. Is there a better way to describe the optimal relationship with God?" No wonder the famous mystics of the Christian tradition would often use sexual imagery to describe their experience of God's presence.

With the church, Gudorf insists that "sexual loving is central to marriage. The friendship and commitment of marriage is conveyed in sexual form. Without the sexual exchange of love and grace, the relationship is not marital."

Lifelong and mutually satisfying sex in marriage requires the dedicated commitment of each partner and the awareness of God's abiding grace. The same is true for the next issue that requires skilled management by both partners — how to handle questions about money and work.

For Reflection

1. *What examples of dualism — splitting the way we think about the human person — do I see in advertising and other places in our society today?*

2. *What connections have I noticed in my life between my physical, mental, and emotional health and well-being?*

3. *What are examples from my own childhood of a lack of proper terminology for genitals?*

4. *What do I think about living together before marriage, and what is the basis for my opinion? What would I want to say to someone who is considering cohabitation?*

5. *If a couple's sexuality is affected by everything in their marriage, what would I predict about the sexuality of a dual-career couple?*

Skill: *I am aware of my attitudes toward and expectations about money and work and am able to talk about them.*

Spend Time and Money Wisely

With their wedding two months away, Amy and Garrett were worried about money. They both had good jobs and good incomes, but they always seemed to be short of money. It looked like they would be forced to take out a loan to pay for some wedding expenses — including the Hawaiian honeymoon they had dreamed about. They had student loans and car loans to pay, and they were borrowing money from Amy's parents for the down payment on a house. They needed to furnish and decorate the house, too. Then there were the monthly minimum payments on their credit cards. Garrett was shocked when he prepared a preliminary monthly budget for their life together. It was several hundred dollars in the red.

Amy and Garrett found themselves fighting when they tried to balance their budget. They discovered that they viewed money very differently and had different financial priorities. Such differences are predictable and troublesome. Money and work can be loaded issues for couples. They need to invest regular time and energy in talking about and becoming aware of the financial needs of their household. Otherwise, they may find themselves "overdrawn" on their ability to make sound major decisions together. When spouses list areas of conflict, financial problems are usually near the top. But often, those fights are not really about money, as we will see.

What we understand money and work to *mean* makes a major difference in the discussions we have about these topics. Our family of origin plays a major role in fashioning this understanding. For example, was money and work discussed in my family of origin, or did it rarely come up? Was there a great deal of money, or was money scarce? How important was comparison shopping or finding a bargain? Who controlled the finances? If only one person handled the money, how knowledgeable about the finances were the other adults in the household? How were credit cards used? How were allowances and loans handled? What experiences did I have of working and handling my own money as a young child and a teenager? Answers to these questions give us a better understanding of what money and work mean to us as adults and equip us to understand what our issues are around money and work as a couple.

Generally speaking, our perspectives on money and work will be similar to those of our family of origin, or they will be intentionally opposite. Unless we examine these perspectives, however, we are not aware of what money and work mean for us now.

Money, for example, may somehow represent power, freedom, independence, success, security, affection, self-respect, anxiety, survival, or other needs or values. Psychologist and economist Joseph Margolin says that "money has always been a substitute for the real thing — whatever that might be — in our lives and in our arguments." If, therefore, money means success to me, and if what I do doesn't result in much income, then I may feel like a failure. Or if I associate money with power, I will feel powerless if I wield little influence on the family budget.

Kathryn Stechert, in "Why You Fight about Money" (*Better Homes and Gardens*, August 1986), says that money fights are often about something other than money. She cautions couples, "The danger in using money as a scapegoat is twofold: the issues behind the money feuds aren't faced, and the money matters aren't resolved. Both problems fester and eventually erode the relationship. Ending financial battles begins with learning to recognize when money is a mask for something else." Stechert offers several key behaviors that help couples determine if they are actually fighting about money or if some other issue is at the core of their disagreement:

- when you keep having the same argument over and over with a predicable outcome;

- when fights about other topics veer quickly to money topics;
- when a fight about money evokes an unreasonable emotional response;
- when comments about the other person's skill as a money manager or earner keep coming into the fight.

These behaviors, according to Stechert, should alert people to the fact that they are not actually struggling with money but are struggling, rather, with some other issue that is behind the money disagreement.

How can couples avoid problems with money and its various meanings? Honest talking and responsible planning are the main ways to keep this topic from being a problem. I suggest that couples develop a money language that allows them to use words like *want* and *need* in the same way, that couples plan to talk about money when it isn't a pressing issue, and that couples review the chapter "Skill Five: Communicate Effectively" (page 75) in light of their discussion about money. I especially encourage people to seek the help of professionals in financial planning and credit counseling when needed.

Making a Living

It's also helpful to understand the cultural ideas we harbor about what money and work mean. Knowing how the economic life of our country has affected marriage and family life in the past three centuries helps us see how we got to where we are today. We know historically, for example, that love was not always — and at times isn't today — the basis for marriage, but we don't often stop to see how the way a family makes its living can shape more than its financial well-being.

In the eighteenth century, ours was primarily an agricultural society. Much of what families needed was produced on family farms, which was where more than 90 percent of the population lived. This meant spouses and children worked side by side to provide for their daily needs. While life was often very hard, the family had control of much of its life, from education to health care. There was a great deal of interdependent work, and children — who were an economic asset — were responsible at an early age and could learn skills from their parents and other elders.

By the nineteenth century, industrialization began to change the face of the American family. Economic pressures drew families away from their farms and into towns and cities, where Dad became a worker in the factory, while Mom and kids — who were becoming financial liabilities — stayed home. (In a number of ethnic groups, of course, Mom and the kids also entered the workforce.) Because the gulf between work and home widened, it became increasingly difficult for parents to train their children for this new world. While designed to support the family, other emerging institutions, such as formal education and health care, began to complicate the picture further.

By the twentieth century, technological advances such as the telephone, the automobile, radio and television, and the development of plastics affected the family even further. The mobility of this century alone has had a big effect on family life in terms of a breakdown of the community of the extended family and neighborhood and the supports that those offered to families. Although women have worked outside the home at various times in our history, the magnitude of this shift in the late twentieth century has had a major impact on how we view family roles and what we can expect from families.

Today, what do we expect from family life and the way we make a living? How does relocating, for example, or having to put in too many hours at work or being unhappy at a job or unemployed affect the family? When we spend the most productive part of our day at our work or studies, what's left for the most important people in our lives at the end of the day? And although there are signs that information technology may be allowing us to work from home more flexibly than in the past, what about the temptation, then, to work more hours instead of "coming home" at the end of the day?

SPEND TIME AND MONEY WISELY

What does work and the money it produces mean to each of us? Is it, for example, an end in itself or a tool? When one of us makes more money than the other, does that somehow mean that person's job is more important? What does it say about our society when some of the most important "people" jobs, like teaching and child care, are some of the lowest paid positions? What about our workplaces, where women are paid an average of seventy-four cents for every dollar that men are paid? (The good news is that the wage differential is slowly improving.)

Planning Our Use of Money

The key word here is *our*. Because money and work are such critical issues for a couple, joint planning and handling of resources is essential. To help plan responsibly and spend with discipline, I suggest that every couple consider the following questions:

- Is it my money and your money, or is it our money?
- How well do we budget what we spend?
- Who pays the bills, or can we sit down together and pay them so that we both know what's going where each month?
- How does each of us handle credit, establishing a decent credit rating for major purchases but not abusing credit as a tool?

- What spending habits do each of us have?
- Are there significant differences between what we each see as a need and a want?
- Do we agree on what constitutes a major purchase, an amount above which we will check with the other before spending?
- When we don't agree on a major purchase — especially when it seems irrational to one of us — do we see how the issues of power, freedom, independence, success, security, affection, self-respect, anxiety, survival, or image may be influencing our judgment?
- How do or will we handle checking and savings accounts — joint or separate — and are we satisfied with how they are set up?
- What insurance and investments do we want to consider as we look ahead and plan for our children's education and our retirement years?

There are many ways to answer each of these questions and many ways that a couple can work out finances and job issues. I cannot stress too strongly that this is an area where a husband and wife need to work together. If it is, in fact, *our* money, then we *both* need to know what's being earned and how it's being spent. I am always concerned when I see couples who do not combine their money to form a single budget, because when one spouse can't trust the other financially, I wonder what that says about the rest of their relationship.

A Christian Perspective on Money

A Christian set of values, which sees people as more important than things, is a radical perspective in a culture obsessed with money. We hear it all the time: "Time is money" and "Money talks" and "What's it worth?" In the face of this cultural obsession with money and goods, in a society that urges us to have more, do more, and go faster, we fail to raise the radical question, "How much is enough?" Are we more than just what we have or what we do, as is often implied in our culture? Because the United States constitutes a mere 4.6 percent of the world's population yet consumes more than 20 percent of the planet's resources, "How much is enough?" is indeed a countercultural and urgent question. When we have to insure, maintain, repair, and replace so much stuff, while millions of people around the globe don't even have the basic things needed to lead dignified human lives, we bear a tremendous moral responsibility to answer this question with caution and courage.

In an interview in *Our Sunday Visitor*, John Kavanaugh, S.J., observes that a great deal of pressure is being used to "teach people to relate less and less to human beings and invest more and more of our life and love into objects. Paradoxically, we treat objects more and more personally and treat others more and more impersonally."

Gospel values tell us that all we have is a gift from God, who is our true security. All our resources — time, energy, talent, money — are gifts given to us for the good of others. As the document *The Pastoral Constitution on the Church in the Modern World* from Vatican II reminds us:

> In his use of things man should regard the external goods he legitimately owns not merely as exclusive to himself but common to others also, in the sense that they can benefit others as well as himself. (n. 69)

In other words, we are stewards of what we have — not owners. Even though we work hard to earn what we have, a sense of stewardship about our possessions and abilities means we make them available for the common good of all. In a Catholic Christian marriage, this means that volunteering our time, energy, and talents and making charitable contributions to enhance and enrich the lives of others are a part of our discussions about how we spend our time and money. For example, Chris and Stephanie find that spending time with the local Habitat for Humanity project helps them to see how other people in their community are forced to live. It also gives them a chance to meet people whose values are similar to theirs.

The Christian perspective on money should be helpful to couples like Amy and Garrett as they decide how to make financial decisions in their marriage. In fact, they may well find that being Christian changes many things about their marriage. In the deepest sense, marriage unites their spirits.

For Reflection

1. *How do I see job issues affecting a couple I know?*
2. *If I could choose to live in the eighteenth-, nineteenth-, or twentieth-century family, which would I choose and why?*
3. *How do I see credit as a tool? How could it end up being destructive?*
4. *What are the advantages and disadvantages to one spouse's paying the bills versus both spouses' being involved in that process together?*
5. *What is an example of the value of charity or service in my experience or that of someone I know?*

Skill: *I am able to articulate my own beliefs and spirituality and to respect the spirituality of others.*

Grow in the
Spiritual Life

As their relationship has deepened, Ben and Janelle have avoided discussing one thing — their Christian faith. Ben is an active Lutheran; Janelle is a fervent Catholic. They've avoided the issue because they're not sure what they might find if they probe too deeply. Each knows very little about the other's faith tradition. Neither of them has much experience explaining their beliefs to someone else. But, as their parents keep reminding them, Lutherans and Catholics are different. How different? Different enough to threaten their relationship? What faith would they share if they married? How would they raise their children? Faith and spirituality are so important to Ben and Janelle that they realize that they can't put off talking about them much longer.

When a couple begins to consider marriage, as Ben and Janelle are, the "meaning-of-life questions" deeply rooted in every human being begin to press to the surface. Is there a God, for example? Does God, as I understand God, have anything to do with the presence of this other person in my life? If God is love, as the first letter of John tells me, then does the love of this person for me, and the love we share, show me something of what and who God is in my life — and our life?

These questions bring up issues of spirituality and religion. For an increasing number of people, spirituality and religion are not the same thing. *Spirituality,* for example, is often used to describe "the way I live in light of what I believe." *Religion,* on the other hand, usually means "a set of practices and traditions that have originated with a group of believers and that are intended to express and nurture that group's spirituality."

Too often, however, spirituality and religious practices do not coincide. Many people today, for example, are aware of and comfortable with their spirituality but, at the same time, search for a religious practice that is suitable and relevant to their spirituality. There are also those people who participate in a well-defined religious practice but find it somehow disconnected from their spirituality. For individuals considering marriage, this disparity can complicate discussions about faith, spirituality, and religion. Unfortunately, the problem often rests in a lack of understanding regarding one's personal beliefs, and the inability to find a common language to talk about spirituality and religion.

GROW IN THE SPIRITUAL LIFE

We can use signs and symbols to help us think through and talk about this complex topic.

Signs and Symbols

In the chapter "The Catholic Vision of Marriage" (page 11), I discussed the Catholic vision of marriage as a sacrament, noting that sacraments are signs of God's invisible, intangible love and grace. As human beings, we are sign-making and symbol-making creatures. We use signs and symbols to say the unsayable when the spoken word seems to lack the power and clarity to express what we know or feel. Within our human relationships, we use greeting cards, presents, notes, and special gestures to let others know how special they are to us.

For example, when Jon and Heather had been dating for a year, Jon gave Heather a small model Volkswagen and a toy powerboat. To the casual observer, these two toys appear meaningless — even silly. But Heather "heard" exactly what Jon was trying to express: he deeply appreciated the many good talks they'd shared over the year in Heather's little bug, and he valued their special times on his family's boat. For Heather and Jon, those simple objects capture and express something that they would otherwise have a hard time articulating. They are precious because of the stories that give them meaning.

If you were to gather objects that communicate who you are and what your life has meant, what would you assemble?

GROW IN THE SPIRITUAL LIFE

Perhaps you would include photographs, certain toys, pieces of jewelry, or items from nature that represent experiences that have had special meaning to you. Each item, and your collection as a whole, however, will have little meaning or real value to others because they don't know the stories that make each keepsake special.

Communities and individuals need signs and symbols to operate well. Traffic signs, money, flags, uniforms, corporate logos, and songs — these are some of the signs and symbols human beings use to define, explain, and organize life, and we too often take them for granted. Yet without a common story, or at least a general agreement, regarding what the symbols mean — money, for example — they cease to serve the community or the individual in a constructive fashion. Simply put, they lose their meaning.

What does this human need to use signs and symbols have to do with spirituality and religion? When we deal with the completely unsayable mysteries of what life means, we need the power of signs and symbols to make tangible what we cannot otherwise grasp. The cross, for example, is a powerful symbol for Christians, capturing the awe and mystery of redemptive pain, salvation, and eternal life. We use things like icons, statues, medals, and other blessed objects to communicate what we believe. We also use images connected to our senses when we talk about the experience of faith; we talk, for example, about being "enlightened" or being "cleansed" of our sins.

Through the centuries, the Catholic tradition has developed seven signs, or events, that make tangible and celebrate its life of faith as a Christian community. These are called sacraments. Sacraments are visible, tangible signs of an invisible, intangible reality: God's love. Sacraments engage our senses, yet go beyond all that we can touch, taste, see, smell, and hear, to say the unsayable. Although other Christian traditions share some of these sacraments, especially baptism, the Catholic tradition has celebrated seven sacraments for much of its history and teaches that God's love is celebrated in each one.

I believe that the sacraments invite us to celebrate different facets, or aspects, of the invisible and intangible reality of God's love.

- Baptism celebrates God's *welcoming* love, calling those being baptized to journey with the community of believers into dying and rising with Jesus.

- Confirmation celebrates God's *strengthening,* or confirming, love, a love that helps those being confirmed to live the commitment they've made in baptism, relying on the gifts of the Holy Spirit.

- Eucharist, or communion, celebrates God's *nourishing* love in the signs of bread and wine, giving sustenance to those who receive the very body and blood — the life — of Jesus.

- Reconciliation, or confession, celebrates God's *forgiving* love, a love that joyfully takes us back when we turn away from God and others and encourages us to reform our lives.
- Holy orders, or ordination, is a celebration of being called to share God's *serving* love with the whole community, a love Jesus modeled when he washed the disciples' feet at the Last Supper.
- The anointing of the sick, sometimes called the last rites because it used to be given only in danger of death, celebrates God's *healing* love, a healing that can be both spiritual and physical.
- Matrimony celebrates God's *lifelong commitment* in love, a love that allows the couple to promise "forever."

Marriage actually seems to celebrate — through the couple's love — all of these aspects of God's love: God's welcoming, strengthening, nourishing, forgiving, serving, and healing love.

Specifically, the married couple is a visible, tangible sign of God's love in at least three ways. First, the husband and wife are a sign — although not perfect — of God's love *to each other*. In their efforts to accept each other and to cherish and delight in each other, they are signs of what God's love looks like and who God is. In his homily at our wedding, the priest who witnessed my marriage to Mitch put it this way: "There have been many people in both of your lives who have been the tangible experience of God's love for you, but now each of you needs to be the main way that the other knows God's love."

Second, since their love is for more than each other, the two are also a sign of God's love *to others*. That includes those who watch the couple's relationship early on, wondering if real love is possible or if the relationship is too good to be true. As the years go by, these others will include people in their respective families and faith communities, as well as their neighbors, friends, and children. All will watch this love unfold year after year. The couple's love, like God's, is a generative love, a love that helps make more love. The *Catechism of the Catholic Church* discusses holy orders and matrimony together, describing them as sacraments directed toward the salvation of others: "If they contribute as well to personal salvation, it is through service to others that they do so. They confer a particular mission in the Church and serve to build up the People of God" (n. 1535).

Finally, the spouses are a sign of God's love *because of others* in their lives, most of whom gather on their wedding day to witness the "yes" they give each other. That "yes" is only possible because of the "yeses" that others have said to them throughout their lives, "yeses" that have helped bring them to this very celebration of love. The couple continues to need support from others in order to be a reflection of God's love through the years. As I mentioned in the chapter

GROW IN THE SPIRITUAL LIFE

"The Catholic Vision of Marriage" (page 11), the community needs to be there to support them.

In their vows as the ministers of this sacrament to each other, the bride and groom promise their future, no matter what that may be. Together, they embark on an adventure, a process, that is more marry*ing* each other than being marr*ied* to each other. Only God knows what their future may hold and what graces they will need. Because their covenant is based on God's enduring love, however, they can say yes to a future neither of them can fully imagine.

The sacrament of marriage is not some magical thing that happens to two people on their wedding day, however. As Raymond Hunthausen, former archbishop of Seattle, explains in *Pastoral Letter on Matrimony* (July 1982), the sacrament of marriage is "not so much something that a couple *receives* as something that a couple *becomes*" (italics added). Day by day, through diapers and dishes, garbage and gardens, feast and famine, the grace of the sacrament of matrimony allows the husband and wife to see their entire life together as holy. As a marriage, their relationship now becomes the main way of living out their Christian faith, and the most religious activity either of them can be about is being good spouses to each other.

Looking at marriage as a sacrament, and realizing the holiness of everyday family life (which we will explore in the next chapter), is not the same as the fairy-tale notion of living happily ever after. It does not mean that our days will be brilliant with bliss and our nights full of passion. Rather, the sacrament of matrimony means that we face whatever life brings, knowing we are graced with a strength beyond ourselves and a different vision of who we are and what we are about. In his excellent book titled *Beginning Your Marriage,* author John L. Thomas describes this vision of marriage in terms of what the bride and groom say to those gathered at their wedding, when they state their vows:

> We believe with you in the glorious Christian vision, . . . the impossible dream that says if we pour our lives out for each other, we will possess them more richly. We have the courage to try to imitate the Gospel love story in our lives. We want you to look at us, to be inspired, to take heart, for we are willing to hazard ourselves in the deep faith that this vision is true, that it is what life is really about, and that it is the way we will find fulfillment here and hereafter.

Marriage in Scripture

Scripture helps us to see the holiness of married love in many ways. The chapters "The Catholic Vision of Marriage" (page 11) and "Skill Seven: Get Comfortable with Sex" (page 101) mentioned the powerful vision from the first chapter of Genesis, which emphasizes the importance of our sexuality and the longing for intimacy within each of us. Being male

and female — not just one or the other — is how we are
made in the image of God. It is in the intimacy between us,
Genesis reminds us, that we know God.

The second chapter of Genesis — a separate and
probably older creation account, according to most Scripture
scholars — describes the relationship between male and
female in another way. In verse 7 we read, "Then the LORD
God formed man from the dust of the ground, and breathed
into his nostrils the breath of life; and the man became
a living being."

The Hebrew word for "man" — here neither male nor
female — is *ha adam,* and this human is made from the *ha
adama,* the earth. What brings this "earth creature" into existence, the passage tells us, is the *ruah* of God, a Hebrew word
that can mean "wind," "breath," or "spirit" — any air in motion. This is the same *ruah* that swept over the face of the
waters before creation in the first chapter of Genesis. Because
God knows that it is not good for the human to be alone
(verse 18), the human names all the animals and birds, which
shows the human's power over them in Hebrew culture. But
the human is still lonely until "the LORD God caused a deep
sleep to fall upon the man, and he slept; then he took one of
his ribs and closed up its place with flesh. And the rib that the
LORD God had taken from the man he made into a woman
and brought her to the man. Then the man said, 'This at last is
bone of my bones and flesh of my flesh; this one shall be called
Woman, for out of Man this one was taken'" (verses 21 – 23).

For the first time in this passage we now have gender, and the woman *(issa)* is taken from the side of the man *(is),* just as the human *(adam)* came from the earth *(adama).* In one another the humans now find the equal partner that they long for. The attitude of respect and equality between the sexes that we see in these passages is especially impressive when we consider that it was written in the midst of a highly patriarchal culture, where women were basically considered property and where the main goal of marriage was passing on the family name through children.

In the third chapter of Genesis, however, we hear about tensions and inequality between the sexes: "To the woman [God] said, 'I will greatly increase your pangs in childbearing; in pain you shall bring forth children, yet your desire shall be for your husband, and he shall rule over you'" (verse 16). This condition is a result of the disobedience and loss of innocence based on the human choice to eat from the fruit of the forbidden tree; it is not what God intended for men and women, as we saw in the first and second chapters of Genesis.

Marriage and wedding imagery is used by various prophets throughout the Old Testament to describe the tenderness and delight of God toward the people of Israel. Isaiah 62:5 reminds us, "As the bridegroom rejoices over the bride, so shall your God rejoice over you." The theme of sensual delight in the beloved and longing for the other is central also in the Song of Solomon, where we read, "I am my beloved's, and his desire is for me" (7:10). Using the vivid language of

141

Hebrew love poetry, this Old Testament book tells us of God's longing for us and God's delight in us. In other passages in the Prophets, such as Ezekiel 16, the image of marriage is used to talk about Israel — the "wife" — being unfaithful and refusing to follow the commandments and the covenant with God. Even then, Yahweh could never give up on her.

The theme of the unfaithful wife is also key to the prophecy of Hosea: "When the Lord first spoke through Hosea, the Lord said to Hosea, 'Go, take for yourself a wife of whoredom and have children of whoredom, for the land commits great whoredom by forsaking the Lord'" (1:2). But God's message through the prophet is always one of mercy and forgiveness: "I will take you for my wife forever; I will take you for my wife in righteousness and in justice, in steadfast love, and in mercy. I will take you for my wife in faithfulness; and you shall know the Lord" (Hosea 2:19–20). When the prophets want to tell the people about God's tender, forgiving love that delights in the beloved, they often use the human experience of married love.

When we turn to the New Testament, we see Jesus exemplifying the tone of respect and equality that we saw in the first two chapters of Genesis, in both his unusually comfortable relationships with women and his strong teachings about marriage. When asked about divorce, Jesus is aware that some Jewish authorities see divorce as permissible, but he responds, quoting Genesis, "From the beginning of creation, 'God made them male and female. For this reason a man shall leave his father and mother and be joined to his wife, and the two shall become one flesh.' So they are no longer two, but one flesh. Therefore what God has joined together, let no one separate" (Mark 10:6 – 9). When his disciples ask him about this, he responds in a way that emphasizes women's obligations as well as men's — even though a woman's initiation of divorce, at that time, was almost unknown. He says to them, "Whoever divorces his wife and marries another commits adultery against her; and if she divorces her husband and marries another, she commits adultery" (Mark 10:11 – 12). While Jesus seems to be compassionate when dealing with those who don't live up to this ideal, like the Samaritan woman at the well (John 4), he strongly defends the value and permanence of marriage.

After Jesus' death, Paul talks about the holiness of marriage in his letters to the early Christian communities. When Paul talks about marriage and family life, he usually does so in the context of describing the whole household and how it should look "in Christ," which is how he saw everything. He writes to the community at Colossae:

> Wives, be subject to your husbands, as is fitting in the Lord. Husbands, love your wives and never treat them harshly. Children, obey your parents in everything, for this is your acceptable duty in the Lord. Fathers, do not provoke your children, or they may lose heart. Slaves, obey your earthly masters in everything, not

only while being watched and in order to please them, but wholeheartedly, fearing the Lord. Whatever your task, put yourselves into it, as done for the Lord and not for your masters, since you know that from the Lord you will receive the inheritance as your reward; you serve the Lord Christ. (Colossians 3:18 – 24)

Notice the hierarchy implicit in Paul's comments. Most strikingly, we can see this in the master-slave relationship, but according to Paul, the same is true of husband-wife and parent-child relationships.

While Paul is aware of the freedom of the gospel, in which "there is no longer Jew or Greek, there is no longer slave or free, there is no longer male and female; for all of you are one in Christ Jesus" (Galatians 3:28), he cannot seem to see past his own culture. For Paul there is no contradiction between accepting an institution like slavery and having a Christian household. Although we now understand slavery as not Christian, this freedom in Christ continues to present a challenge that Christians are still trying to understand how to live out fully.

Similarly, the patriarchal understanding of what marriage is has shifted from Paul's time to our own. We understand now that there is no one way to be married as a Christian and that, for believers, Christ is a part of the couple's relationship day in and day out. The goal for a Christian couple is *mutual* submission, as the U.S. bishops advise couples in their letter to families, titled *Follow the Way of Love:* "A couple who accepts their equality as sons and daughters in the Lord will honor and cherish one another. They will respect and value each other's gifts and uniqueness."

As the letter to the Ephesians reminds us, "Be subject to one another out of reverence for Christ" (5:21).

Interfaith Marriage

We know, as sociologists point out, that our world is, in a way, shrinking. Modern technology and advanced means of transportation have allowed us to meet, work with, and remain in communication with people around the globe. In the past, our world was more limited in terms of geography and communication, which meant that our opportunities for human relating were narrower as well.

This is not the case today. Relationships span the globe, and we have many more opportunities to encounter people from backgrounds quite different from our own. As a result, intermarriage has become much more common, bringing couples together from different age-groups and widely diverse ethnic, faith, cultural, and socioeconomic backgrounds.

In *Building a Successful Intermarriage between Religions, Social Classes, Ethnic Groups, or Races,* Dr. Man Keung Ho, himself in an intercultural marriage, suggests that there are advantages and disadvantages to intermarriage. The advantages include a more thorough preparation for

marriage, a greater degree of commitment to the relationship, a greater degree of self-other differentiation, a greater
degree of acceptance, tolerance, and respect, broader opportunities for learning and growth, and greater opportunities
and acceptance of differences in children. On the other hand,
there can be problems from families, friends, and faith
communities or religious groups. There can even be
discrimination, especially with regard to housing or
employment. Within the couple there can be differences
about food and eating, festivities and observances,
friendships, financial management, sexual attitudes, child
rearing — and spirituality and religion.

When two people from different faith backgrounds form
a marriage, we call it an interfaith marriage. There are three
kinds of interfaith marriages: the *interreligious marriage,* the
interdenominational marriage, and the *intradenominational
marriage.* All involve unique challenges.

An *interreligious marriage* is the marriage of two people
from different belief systems, such as the marriage of a Hindu
and a Buddhist, or a Christian and an atheist. Because the
basic structures of these various belief systems can be so
fundamentally different, people in an interreligious marriage
may struggle to find common ground and common language
for sharing their spirituality and religion.

An *interdenominational marriage* is the marriage of two
Christians who belong to different Christian denominations,
such as Ben and Janelle (mentioned at the beginning of this

146

chapter). While both may believe in the Bible as the Word of God, their respective interpretations of God's word in Scripture may be entirely different — even at odds. They also may have different understandings of what their Christian commitment and church membership mean. This can make certain issues in the marriage — beliefs about marriage, roles, and religious celebrations, for example — complex and painful.

Fortunately, certain segments of the Christian community are joining efforts to support those couples who enter interdenominational marriages. In *Pastoral Letter on Christian Unity* (1978), an interdenominational group of religious leaders in Connecticut stated their perspective on interdenominational marriage this way:

> We advise you to settle as honestly and gently as possible the sensitive questions surrounding the religious education of your children — preferably prior to your marriage. Then show us a love of each other that encourages the other to remain faithful to the best in his or her own tradition. This means that you cannot be ignorant of the religious heritage and worship of your spouse. Lastly, believe that you are doing something new in Christian history. We ask you to accept this challenge as part of the movement of the Holy Spirit to draw us together in Christ. While you carry the pain of religious division, you also carry the promise of

GROW IN THE SPIRITUAL LIFE

Christian unity. We are with you in prayer; be with us in fidelity to your union.

Even with increasing support and respect from all Christian traditions, the interdenominational marriage can be challenging, especially if the couple's respective religious ideologies come to bear on the discipline and religious formation of children.

An *intradenominational marriage* is the marriage of two people from the same Christian denomination: two Catholics, two Methodists, two Baptists. Even with their common background, however, two people in an intradenominational marriage can still face serious issues if there are significant differences in the way each person understands or expresses that background. In fact, profound and potentially perilous spiritual differences between partners from the same denomination are quite common and are often overlooked. Frequently, these differences are far more disruptive to the marriage than are the differences found in interreligious or interdenominational marriages.

Janice, for example, saw her parents struggle with their differences, although both her parents were Catholic. Janice's mother embraced and adhered to the practices of the Catholic Church that predate the Second Vatican Council. Her father's faith, on the other hand, embraced all the developments that have emerged since the council. Her parents' basic understandings of sin, sacrament, and grace were painfully different, causing them severe tension around things like prayer styles, preferences in liturgy, and a common language of faith.

Of course, there is a certain interfaith dimension to any marriage. Because my spirituality is uniquely mine, and my relationship with God is so deeply personal, the way I experience my faith will always — to some degree — differ from another's. But partners with profoundly different spiritual and religious backgrounds and values should embark on marriage with great care and caution.

Religious values — especially differing religious values — become a pressing issue when couples think about becoming parents. But that's only one of the things they have to think about. Let's examine what it takes to be parents.

For Reflection

1. *If I were to make a collection of personal symbols as described early in this chapter, what would I include, and what would be stories that helped make those objects special for me?*

2. *What has been my experience of church attendance, and what does it mean to me? How does church attendance connect to my spirituality?*

3. *What couples do I know who are visible signs of God's invisible love to me? How?*

4. *When I think about marriage as being holy, what are three daily events that are, therefore, holy, even though they may not seem to be?*

5. *How have I seen partners in an interfaith marriage, whether interreligious, interdenominational, or intradenominational, resolve the issues that their differences present?*

Skill: I am open to having children and to the ways that being a parent may tretch me to grow.

Be Open to
Being a Parent

As their wedding day approaches, Susan and Rich often talk about having children. The idea excites them, but it also makes them apprehensive. They like children but fear actually becoming parents. Rich's little nieces and nephews seem like so much fun for his older brother and his wife. But some older children don't seem so pleasant. How would children change their relationship as a couple? Do they really have what it takes to raise a family? Questions like these worry them.

These questions worry every young couple. How does a couple know when the time is right to begin a family? In an article titled "Children: Feed Them on Your Dreams" (*U.S. Catholic*, June 1982), Ron and Jo Ann Liszkowski describe the shift from married love to being parents in this way:

Throughout courtship and the early years of marriage [the couple] learns to be together in a way so intimate it can be found in no other way. They learn to know one another in a way found in no other relationship. And it's surprising how even the callous world will bow to that time, smile at it, allow it to go on, make special accommodations to let it be for them. "After all, they're in love."

It seems selfish of them. But as Jonas Salk says, there is an evolutionary spirit in the nature of life that can only be explained as "selfish generosity." For not long after, a couple's nurtured love finds it can't contain itself, must grow out, must become a gift of life to all time. So the child.

As two people consider beginning their family, they face a number of decisions together. How many children do we want and can we handle? What other factors must be taken into account? How can we be generous about our ability to create new life and yet remain realistic about our resources?

The process of making choices regarding family size and the timing of children is well described in the document *The Pastoral Constitution on the Church in the Modern World* from the Second Vatican Council:

> Married couples should regard it as their proper mission to transmit human life and to educate their children; they should realize that they are thereby

cooperating with the love of God the Creator. . . .
This involves the fulfillment of their role with a sense
of human and Christian responsibility and the formation of correct judgments through docile respect for
God and common reflection and effort; it also involves
a consideration of their own good and the good of
their children already born or yet to come, an ability
to read the signs of the times and of their own situation
on the material and spiritual level, and, finally, an esti-
mation of the good of the family, of society, and of the
Church. It is the married couples themselves who must
in the last analysis arrive at these judgments before
God. (n. 50)

The document then goes on to say that couples need
to follow an informed conscience, one formed by the church's
teaching, which urges generosity in creating new life in the
face of a culture that too rarely values life. When it talks
about marriage as an intimate communion of life and love,
Vatican II reminds us of the intimate connection between a
husband and wife's love and their life-giving ability *(Gaudium
et Spes,* n. 48). Pope John Paul II often mentions this theme,
as he did in an address he gave at the Capitol Mall in Washington, D.C., on October 7, 1979, in which he said, "In order
that Christian marriage may favor the total good and development of the married couple, it must be inspired by the
Gospel, and thus be open to new life — new life to be given

BE OPEN TO BEING A PARENT

and accepted generously." In becoming parents we are called to nothing less than the mystery and awe of being cocreators with God of new life.

Where to Start?

How do a man and a woman start a conversation with each other — even before the wedding — about the topic of children and family and what they want and expect? One helpful place to start is spending time with and around children — together and separately — and observing what happens. How comfortable are we with kids and with what age-groups? How do we feel about being parents ourselves? Do we agree on how to talk with and deal with children?

Couples also need to consider and talk about how they each were raised and what they think of their respective experiences. I often explore this topic with my students by asking them about how well they think their parents did. Most of my twenty-year-old undergraduate students have a hard time picturing themselves as parents. All of them, however, have been on the receiving end of the parenting process and, in retrospect, can reflect on what they saw their parents do especially well and what they saw them do poorly. Each time I lead this process I wish the students' parents could hear what has made an impression on their young adult children.

The students' comments include issues like the importance of trusting children, the value of parental support and

BE OPEN TO BEING A PARENT

being there for games or concerts, and the merits of plenty of responsibility: "My parents made me work for things and didn't give me everything I asked for, so I learned the value of work and of what I had." Others talk about the need for reasonable limits: "I wish my parents had set more limits; my sisters and I 'come unglued' at the least bit of stress." Another common theme in the students' comments is the need not to be compared to one's siblings: "I'm glad my parents didn't compare my brother and me; that was very freeing." Whatever their experience, a perspective on how they were raised is an important component of couples' thinking about the task of being parents.

Couples also need to talk about approaches to discipline — not in detail, but in general terms — so that they have some idea of each other's approach to issues that will come up later. They might even consider taking a parenting class together early in the pregnancy before the childbirth classes. "That way," explains a couple who has recently done just that, "we know that we're on the same wavelength when it comes to how to approach issues as parents." For example, the individuals in a couple need to know if their approach is authoritarian or more permissive, and what they think about spanking as a disciplinary measure. In the midst of so many ideas on parenting, how do the husband and wife use their own common sense and make sure that they are being consistent with each other?

With so many dual-career couples today, another issue that needs much discussion is child care. Who will be home with our children? Will there be a need for supplementary child care and if so, what kind? Are we comfortable with someone other than the two of us having a major impact on our young children?

And what if we find that we are unable to have children? In the face of infertility, are we open to adopting or being foster parents? One young woman told me that she wished someone had encouraged her and her fiancé to talk about that issue years ago, because it became a huge problem later in their marriage. Talking about it before they got married hadn't occurred to them.

Increasingly, some couples may find themselves dealing with a child or children from a previous marriage or relationship. Stepparenting involves a complex adjustment for both the children and adults involved, and patience and clear communication are key. Custody arrangements that have children shuttling from one home environment to another may make the situation even more difficult.

A Foundation for Faith: The Domestic Church

Whatever the specifics of our situation, when we take on the role of parents we become the foundation for our children's worlds in many ways, including their faith formation. Our families are the place where we first begin to understand love, forgiveness, joy, hope, and trust, as well as where we must put our faith and spirituality into practice. If I can love the neighbor — and often the enemy — with whom I share a common roof, then I can love anyone. Families are not always the cozy places pictured in Norman Rockwell paintings, but they are powerful forges of faith.

In *Follow the Way of Love: A Pastoral Message of the U.S. Catholic Bishops to Families,* the bishops had this to say: "A family is our first community and the most basic way in which the Lord gathers us, forms us, and acts in the world. The early church expressed this truth by calling the Christian family a *domestic church* or *church of the home.*"

After naming some of the ways in which families carry out the mission of the whole church in ordinary, everyday ways — by loving each other, fostering intimacy, serving each other, forgiving, celebrating life, and welcoming strangers, for example — the bishops comment, "No domestic church does all of this perfectly. But neither does any parish or diocesan church . . . remember, a family is holy not because it is perfect but because God's grace is at work in it, helping it to set out anew every day on the way of love."

Although the bishops use the word *church,* they obviously don't mean a building, and they don't mean merely the churchy things in a home, like prayer or religious art. They mean primarily a quality of relationship with others in the home that shows itself in spending time together and in serving others, both within the family and outside it. *The Catechism*

BE OPEN TO BEING A PARENT

of the Catholic Church reminds us that "parents have the first responsibility for the education of their children. They bear witness to this responsibility first by creating a home where tenderness, forgiveness, respect, fidelity, and disinterested service are the rule" (n. 2223).

The domestic church within the home also shows itself in times of prayer and celebration that flow from this life together and the countless rituals that celebrate the many naturally holy times in the family, from birthdays to the first day of school to bedtime to the first driver's license. More and more, we understand from secular sources as well as religious ones that our rituals are what help anchor us in a world that is changing too rapidly. We need certain events and actions that we can count on from year to year that will remain basically the same. In those rituals, we celebrate the fact that we are, indeed, a web of relationships within which we experience God's presence. In the *Bringing Religion Home* newsletter, syndicated columnist Ellen Goodman put it this way: "We create our own traditions for the same reasons we create our families: to know where we belong."

This household of faith will also handle issues like parenting and marriage and sexuality in a distinctive way in light of faith, keeping the love of God and one another as clear priorities, not the accumulation of more and more stuff. Ideally, the family as domestic church is both supported and challenged by the local parish in this task. It is supported by the parish's education efforts and other activities that help

BE OPEN TO BEING A PARENT

support the family, yet it is challenged to continue growing as a community in which the good news of God's love is not just talked about but is lived out in practice.

Living out gospel values means that a Christian family may look subtly different than those in the other homes on the block. It may be more critical about violent toys and images in the home or how much television is watched. Hospitality or voluntary service may be a special part of the home. It may also mean that family members are aware of other cultures and of situations of social injustice, more so than other families may be.

Being a domestic church and living out God's love in our daily lives will look different in each family, just as each person's spirituality is unique. The gifts of one household may clearly be those of hospitality, while another household may focus on prayer and ritual. Each home is a place where the good news of love-without-limits is lived in a way that is both real and down-to-earth.

Time for the Marriage

In sharing their lives with children, couples need to make sure that the marriage relationship — which brought them together in the first place and led them to share their love with these children — doesn't get lost. This takes conscious effort on the part of parents. The best single piece of advice my husband, Mitch, and I were given before marriage came from a couple who recommended a weekly date. As a result of that advice, rarely has a week gone by over the past twenty-five years that we haven't gone out — just the two of us — for the evening. We figure the money we have spent on sitters, movies, and so forth is well worth the investment in our relationship. Of course, couples can meet this need in many ways. One couple sets aside one evening a week to turn off the TV, pop popcorn, and just talk.

The questions about sharing their lives with children that we saw Rich and Susan grappling with at the beginning of this chapter have wide implications. In deciding to make a home for our children, we pass on what is most important to us, and in doing that, we recognize more fully the holiness that is always there "where two or more are gathered" in Jesus' name. One of the best examples of God's enduring love that parents can give their children is in the fidelity to our relationship as spouses, to which we now turn.

For Reflection

1. *How have I seen a marriage change with the addition of one or more children?*
2. *What do I notice about myself when I am around children?*
3. *Who do I know who is adopted or has stepparents? How has that experience been for them?*

BE OPEN TO BEING A PARENT

4. *What daily or seasonal rituals are there in my family or one that I know? How do these rituals nourish the spirituality of that family?*

5. *A family that I know that has warm hospitality is _____ . How do I see that family make others feel welcome, and how is that an example of everyday holiness?*

Skill: *I appreciate marriage as a process and as a commitment to change and growth.*

Get Ready to Change and Grow

Greg and Melissa wonder what's gone wrong with their marriage. It's not that their relationship is bad; it just seems dull. They both feel like they've been doing the same things for the past twelve years. Although their two daughters, ages ten and eight, give them a great deal of delight and take up a fair amount of their attention, there doesn't seem to be much left to their marriage but habit. They wonder how their love, once so alive and exciting, can now feel so stifling. Greg and Melissa haven't been willing to talk with each other about these feelings and concerns, because neither knows how to get out of this "stuck" place. Even their faith, which is part of what drew them together in the first place, has become something private and individual for each them, not an experience that holds them together as a couple.

Melissa and Greg are victims of an assumption that afflicts many marriages: that we are marr*ied* rather than marry*ing* each other. Too often, couples think that most of the work is finished once the bills from the wedding have been paid and all the pictures have been shown to the relatives. The fact is, the work — and the joy — is just beginning.

When we talk about marriage as a lifelong commitment, we often focus only on the word *commitment,* which is indeed important. In a society that puts a high value on variety and instant gratification, staying together through the good and not-so-good times is not that easy and is, as we have seen, quite countercultural.

We can't focus on commitment, however without seeing it as lifelong — which implies change. As a living entity, a marriage must change and grow or else it dies. In the novel *The Sparrow,* by Mary Doria Russell, an older woman tells her friend Jimmy about her marriage:

> "I have been married at least four times, to four different men. . . . They've all been named George Edwards but, believe me, the man who is waiting for me down the hall is a whole different animal from the boy I married, back before there was dirt. Oh, there are continuities. He has always been fun and he has never been able to budget his time properly."
>
> "But people change," [Jimmy] said quietly.

"Precisely. People change. Cultures change. Empires rise and fall. . . . Every ten years or so, George and I have faced the fact that we have changed and we've had to decide if it makes sense to create a new marriage between these two new people."

In his book titled *The Trouble Book,* psychologist Eugene Kennedy echoes the same idea when he says that the most practical thing that a married couple can prepare for is change. He adds that love doesn't disappear when it changes.

It evolves and transforms itself, demanding something new of husband and wife, allowing them to discover things they never suspected about each other. The learning that goes along with a man and a woman living closely together is never ended. . . . We must not fool ourselves into believing that we already know everything there is to know about the person we married. We *never* have him (or her) all figured out. . . . There are no tired, old marriages. There are only tired and distracted people who have forgotten how to look at each other.

Wendell Berry, a Kentucky farmer and poet, reflects on how much he's learned from the tough — as well as the good — parts of marriage. In *Other Side* (November/December 1994) he says:

The marriage vow states, "Til death do us part." I believe that's because that is how long it takes to get it "right" — a lifetime. Tanya and I have been married for 37 years. That time has not been a constant delirium of joy and happiness. (I can say that because I am the cause of most of the trouble.) It is sometimes joyful, and sometimes it involves grief.

To think we could slide along and avoid suffering in relationships is preposterous. There is a richness in this suffering — a kind of learning of lessons which are not abstract but known and felt. We don't teach the young that a lot of suffering is negligible. We should. There ought not to be a Band-Aid for every little cut.

Change in a marriage is both a challenge and a gift; it is the pulse of intimate relating, indicating that healthy growth is happening. Steve McCornack and Kelly Morrison — husband and wife — try to stress this with their students in their popular classes at Michigan State University, where they teach Communications 225: "Introduction to Interpersonal Relationships." In an article by Susan Ager *(Detroit Free Press,* reprinted in the *Spokesman-Review,* Tuesday, January 5, 1999), McCornack and Morrison outline nine rules of love, of which they feel number four to be the most important:

1. *Abandon the passion delusion.* Passion declines over time. This is natural and normal, not horrible.

2. *Romantic feelings can't be forced.* You can't talk yourself into falling in love. Nor can you engineer situations to stir passion you don't feel.

3. *Relationships are hard work.* You must constantly put effort into maintaining a relationship, just as you would a career or a car.

4. *Commitment is a process.* Once a commitment is agreed upon, it will not stay alive if it's left alone. The same effort that created the commitment must be invested each and every day.

5. *Maintain independence and solitary outside activities.* Most long-term, vital couples spend a fair amount of time apart from each other, pursuing separate interests and hobbies that fulfill them.

6. *But cultivate mutual interests and activities, too.*

7. *Discuss honesty rules.* Negotiate exactly what you must tell each other — about the past and the present — and what, if anything, is best left unsaid.

8. *Confront conflict.* Many relationships are slowly destroyed as partners avoid discussing issues about which they disagree.

9. *Foster friendship.* A romantic relationship survives when two people get along as friends, day to day, with affection and respect.

Being faithful in a marriage is about understanding, embracing, and growing with the changes that come into the relationship as a living reality. In the same source mentioned above, Eugene Kennedy points out that "fidelity is not keeping an old promise as much as it is discovering what is new and fresh in life together."

The Stages of Life's Passages

When we view marriage as a constant process of marrying each other, we can respect the series of life's passages that we go through in the course of a marriage. Theorists point out that there are at least three main stages to any life passage: *separation, marginality,* and *reintegration.*

In *separation,* something within me or outside of me impels me to leave the status quo. From outside, for example, I may be graduating from college, losing my job as a result of downsizing, or relocating due to health reasons. From within, I may decide to quit school, seek a different job, or move to a friendlier climate. Either way, I am leaving the status quo and separating from that which is in some way familiar to me.

Whether from within or without, this force moves me to a place of *marginality,* where I am in the midst of stress and uncertainty. What was once comfortable and familiar is now gone, and I struggle to find my bearings in the new situation. Besides being a time of risk and vulnerability, this

GET READY TO CHANGE AND GROW

is also a time of tremendous growth, although it's hard to recognize that in the midst of the experience.

With time, however, *reintegration* begins. Life gradually returns to normal as I regain my bearings and claim who and where I am in this new situation. I emerge from this passage and get on with my life.

This three-part process takes shape in marriage in many ways. When a man and a woman become engaged, for example, they begin to sense the separation from families of origin and friends that their impending marriage will mean. Although the stated reason for bridal showers and bachelor parties, for example, is to celebrate the upcoming marriage, such events are really opportunities to say good-bye to relationships as they have existed in the past.

With the wedding comes the beginning of marginality, which traditionally is made less stressful by taking a honeymoon together to begin life as a couple. With time, the newlyweds get used to seeing themselves as spouses; they are reintegrated as a couple.

Another passage is evident when a couple is ready to send a child off to school for the first time. Many parents find themselves grieving the separation and the fact that they will no longer be the primary influence in their child's life. As much as this change needs to happen, it means a shift from the comfortable way things have been. There may be a time of marginality for the whole family, in fact, as everyone adjusts to dealing with particulars of day care or school routines or bus schedules and to being available to listen to the adventures of a child discovering the world beyond. With time, everyone becomes reintegrated and accustomed to the child's new directions that take him or her into an expanding world.

As the marriage grows through various passages in its life cycle, it will predictably go through certain stages in marriage. These stages include establishing marital patterns as a couple, accommodating children into the marriage, developing careers, facing midlife crises, launching children into adulthood, retiring and finding new purpose together, and aging together. This cycle, of course, looks different for each couple, rarely follows a neat and predictable pattern, and can overlap within itself through the years. With each new stage, the spouses' ability to stay in touch with each other will be challenged.

At each new turn, our fidelity as a couple will be built on a clear sense of our own identity and being faithful to our own dreams so that we can be available for intimacy and a faithfulness to each other's dreams. Without a clear sense of identity, I may decide — somewhere through the years — that I just can't risk any further. As a result, I stop growing and changing along with my partner. But when I am free to be vulnerable and to take the risks that growing demands, I can lay down my life for my spouse in a way that, paradoxically, frees both of us to grow with the assurance of our love for each other.

GET READY TO CHANGE AND GROW

Love versus Law

Much of what can sustain a marriage through the stages of life's passages rests in the overall atmosphere a man and a woman establish early in their relationship, basing their relationship on generosity (love) rather than focusing on everything being "even" (law). In an article titled "How to Get More Married Each Day" (*U.S. Catholic*, June 1979), author Mary Carson clearly describes the difference between love and law: "Love is giving freely, expecting nothing in return. Law concerns itself with an equitable exchange, *this for that*." During childhood, most of us develop a strong sense of law; it's that which leads us to complain, "But it's not fair." Carson describes the contrast between these two stances in marriage in the following example:

> Suppose a husband is delayed coming home from work. What happens? As far as the wife is concerned, by law, she's annoyed that she must keep dinner waiting. With love, she's concerned that he's had to work late. By law, she wonders if he's really working or out having a good time while she's stuck home taking care of the kids and the dead dinner. With love, she's afraid he's had an accident and that's why he hasn't called. By law, if he'd had an accident the police would have called. With love, she knows he's doing the best he can.
>
> How does the husband react? By law, he knows he's not a child; he shouldn't have to account for where he

is every minute. With love, he doesn't want her to worry. By law, he knows he's trying to finish a job at the office. He doesn't know how long he's going to be, so what's he going to tell her if he does call? With love, he calls and makes a date with her. "Why don't you feed the kids and get them to bed, and maybe we can have supper alone when I get home." By law, why should he bother calling; she's already angry anyway.

Carson points out that we are rarely consistent; we often fluctuate back and forth between the two positions, especially with today's more dual-career and egalitarian roles in marriage. ("It's your turn to empty the dishwasher!") But if we go back to the example and look at just the reactions based on love, how much more pleasant and smooth the evening — and the marriage in general — can be!

Another way to understand faithfulness in marriage is to explore its opposite. Being *un*faithful in marriage can encompass much more than the sexual infidelity that usually comes to mind. Whenever anything becomes more important in my life than my spouse, I am being unfaithful. There are, in fact, many ways to be unfaithful, whether it's sports, hobbies, a career, or charitable activities. I can, in a sense, commit adultery with my golf game, for example. I can even be unfaithful to the marriage by taking on the role of parent to the neglect of my spouse. Whenever children — or anything or anyone else — become more important to me than the relationship

I have with my spouse, I am unfaithful to my marriage.

This is not to say that sexual infidelity is a minor infraction; it can, in fact, be one of the most painful experiences ever to challenge a marriage. I suggest, however, that sexual infidelity, while never excusable, is often a symptom of marital problems, rather than a cause. When faced with the pain of sexual infidelity, a couple does well to look at what's happening in the marriage relationship as a whole — not just what's happened outside the marriage. When both spouses are willing to admit that they bear some responsibility for what *wasn't* happening in the marriage, and both are willing to work on the relationship with outside help, their marriage may survive this major challenge. Forgiveness and hope, of course, must be part of this immense challenge.

The Cycle of Marital Intimacy

In any marriage — and in any relationship — difficult times need to be faced if real intimacy is to evolve. The cycle of intimacy at work in a relationship has much to teach us. In an outstanding book titled *Marital Intimacy: A Catholic Perspective,* now sadly out of print, Joan Anzia and Mary Durkin discuss the results of a unique colloquium where the participants described their professional and personal insights on intimacy in marriage. Participants identified four main stages in the process of intimacy — stages that,

GET READY TO CHANGE AND GROW

for most couples, happen over and over again in the course of a marriage.

The first of these is the stage of *falling in love,* when energies within us are aroused by the attractiveness of the other person in a way that lifts us out of the everyday world, shatters our complacency, and brings us face-to-face with Mystery. According to Anzia and Durkin:

> This other is offering us a glimpse of the meaning of life. He or she becomes a sacrament for us, awakening us to the need to move outside ourselves if we want to experience love. Falling in love is a deeply religious experience. We rediscover God's plan for creation. No wonder it is so wonderful.
>
> Not only are we struck with the goodness and "perfection" of the other, he or she begins to help us see our own goodness, as well.
>
> The awareness that another feels we are special and irresistible is very exhilarating. How wonderful to realize that someone thinks that way about us! We see ourselves anew in our lover's eyes. We see the reflection of our unqualified goodness and desirability — and we want to believe it's true.

While falling in love gives us a great high, however, we cannot sustain it forever. Sooner or later we end up *settling down,* which is the second stage of intimacy. We begin to see each other's imperfections and the differences between us, whether in our biological clocks or in our emotional needs. The daily routine begins to intrude, and the risks that being vulnerable to each other demand may seem too high. Anzia and Durkin quote one couple who described settling down:

> Somewhere in those early years, a sourness crept in. We still had a good deal to talk about, but we also had a good deal of daily business to transact, business about the carburetor and the carpenter and lists of names for the cocktail party and of items for the tax man. Every night before the intimacies, there was a pile of messages to exchange and pieces of paper to get out of the way. In retrospect, it seems we rarely got to the intimacies.

From settling down, things seem to get worse before they get better, as the little irritating things about each of us finally begin to get under our skin. Through clenched teeth we realize that we're *bottoming out.* This stage is a time of pain, alienation, fear, and grief—a time of the cross. As Anzia and Durkin put it:

> Together we fear that the hurt between us is beyond repair, the vast gulf between us is beyond forgiveness. We are not good enough for the task. We have gone too far. Together we are overcome by a sinking sensation, a sickening, visceral realization that the relationship may never, ever be the same again.

We are hiding in the garden. We are in exile in
Babylon. It is Good Friday. We are the disciples who
have run away in fear.

As we bottom out, we are faced with a choice. We can address the difficulties that we're experiencing with each other
and risk upsetting the security of our relationship, or we can
let things ride and not talk about what's really happening.

If we choose to let things ride, we will find ourselves
going through the motions of intimacy while becoming satisfied with mediocrity. The subtle numbness that sets in will
leave us willing to face only those minor skirmishes that dis-
turb the surface of the relationship, while we ignore or avoid
the serious problems between us. Although neither of us may
physically leave the relationship, we "check out" emotionally.
Years later, a major event like a serious accident, death, or the
departure of the last child may finish off our relationship,
which really died years earlier.

The other option, of course — talking about what's
really wrong — means a lot of messiness. It begins with setting aside my tendency to blame the other for the problems
and realizing that I'm part of the problem as well.

If a husband and wife choose to fight it out with each
other, rather than hiding or leaving, they are on their way to
beginning again. One of the ways spouses may be drawn back
toward each other is through their mutual sexual attraction,
which the authors liken to a rubber band, often allowing the

GET READY TO CHANGE AND GROW

couple to stretch apart but not fall apart. Anzia and Durkin say that when we begin again

> we know we cannot go back to the same thing.
> We must begin again or draw further apart, and
> the choices are more apparent to us now than
> they were when we first experienced romantic
> love. Then it seemed that the grace of our sexual
> drive was so overpowering that we had little choice.
> God does not directly intervene in our relationship
> now; rather we experience our sexual attraction
> as a renewal of the initial invitation to respond
> to the divine lure to beauty.

Beginning again is a time of hope and resurrection, a time of new life and possibilities. It leads a couple to the stage of falling in love all over again. Being willing to reconcile and forgive — themselves and each other — the two are once again caught up in the splendor of Mystery, where they can begin to love the real person who is their life partner, not just the idea of love.

This cycle of intimacy may happen once or daily in a marriage. It is not so much an unchanging circle as it is a spiral that draws us deeper into intimacy with each other and with God, whose love is at the heart of our love for each other — and others.

How can a couple keep marriage alive and growing as it goes through this cycle of intimacy? Psychologist Eugene

GET READY TO CHANGE AND GROW

Kennedy, quoted earlier, offers two excellent suggestions. He encourages couples:

> Resolve to do something special every day for the one you married. This doesn't take much. It doesn't mean a big present. It means a little thoughtfulness — something done freely rather than out of obligation. It should be the kind of thing that comes as a surprise and carries the message, "You are treasured and loved because you are special."
>
> Do something different once a week and do it together. Do things that bring you into the realm of new experiences and break the grip of routine and dullness. The cost of these adventures need not be high. They are, in fact, priceless because they provide the kind of setting in which people can revitalize their life together.

Marriage is, indeed, a process of life. As it grows through the stages of life's passages and the cycles of marital intimacy, it draws a couple into the deepest experiences of intimacy. When the skills we've been exploring — a clear sense of self, a capacity for love and intimacy, personal maturity, an understanding of one's family of origin, an ability to communicate well, an awareness of gender-role issues, healthy sexual attitudes, responsible financial attitudes, spiritual awareness, openness to children, and appreciation of marriage as a process — are engaged through these stages and cycles, the harvest is abundant. The fruit of a countercultural and

GET READY TO CHANGE AND GROW

sacramental marriage is the experience of a love that is more than we could have dreamed of— one that shows us the awesome face of God.

In the next chapter, I offer a brief review of these critical skills and a blessing prayer for you as you seek — and find — the joys of marriage.

For Reflection

1. *Can I explain the built-in tension in the phrase* lifelong commitment?

2. *What ways of being unfaithful in marriage have I seen, other than sexual infidelity?*

3. *Do I agree or disagree with the statement that there are times when sexual infidelity may be a symptom rather than a cause of problems in a marriage — and at times may be forgivable? Why?*

4. *How does the contrast between love and law take shape in one of my personal relationships?*

5. *Name at least three transitions or passages in the process of a marriage. How well have I seen a couple handle any of these transitions?*

GET READY TO CHANGE AND GROW

Skills Review and
Blessing Prayer

The previous chapters have been specific about the skills and graces needed for a lifelong and satisfying marriage. The following skills review will help you raise issues for further consideration, as an individual or as a couple.

As an Individual

Write your answers to each question. At the end of the skills review, note a specific future date when you will return to this tool to see how, if at all, you have changed. You may want to choose a date that's easy to remember, like a birthday or anniversary. I suggest you plan your review for no more than three to six months in the future.

If you aren't satisfied with your responses in a particular area, reread the chapter involving that skill. You might also check "Suggested Reading" (page 207) for specific titles dealing with that area.

As a Couple

Write responses for yourself and your partner. Then compare your responses to see how well you know what your partner thinks or feels about these topics. It may be helpful to do this when you become engaged, near the time of an anniversary, or with other couples as part of a marriage enrichment session. Be sure to give yourselves time to talk about your responses; it may easily take more than one sitting. Don't forget to note the date and agree on a future date when you will look over your responses again.

Should your responses and discussions indicate that you'd like to find out more about a specific area, refer to the suggested reading list. The appendix (page 194) suggests more complete inventories and other resources for marriage preparation and enrichment.

Skills Review

Skill: I know myself well as loved by God, I like who I am, and I am comfortable with times of solitude.

1. How would I describe myself to someone who's never met me?

2. What five words describe my gifts and positive qualities? What five words describe my faults or shortcomings? Which of these two sets of words was easier to think of?

3. Is it more important to me what others think of me or what I think of myself?

4. Are there certain aspects about myself that I want to change? What are those aspects and why do I want to change them?

5. Do I enjoy spending time alone, or do I dread it and make sure there is noise around if I have to be alone?

6. Do I plan time to be alone? Am I more renewed and energized after spending time by myself?

7. Do I appreciate others' needs for time alone, or do I feel rejected when they don't want to be with me at those times?

Skill: I understand what real love is and have a capacity for personal intimacy.

1. Who knows what I really think and feel about my life?

2. Am I able to let others get close to me, or am I uncomfortable letting anyone know my deepest joys, concerns, and fears, only wanting to have a good time with friends?

3. Can I share my feelings with others, or am I comfortable sharing only thoughts and opinions?

4. Do others see me as dependable, as someone they can count on when needed?

5. Whom do I really trust?

6. In what ways do I love "with a limp," based on my history? Does that ever get in the way of my present relationships?

Skill: *I am personally mature. I have accurate life assumptions, psychological autonomy and maturity, a clear set of values, and an understanding of and capacity for responsibility and commitment.*

1. What are the most important values in my life? How well do I act in accord with those values? Would others who know me well agree with my list?

2. Am I patient with those aspects of my life that take time and don't happen immediately?

3. Am I able to evaluate others accurately as friends? Do others generally agree with me?

4. Can I stay with what I begin and see it through to completion? Can I sacrifice, if need be, to attain a goal I set for myself?

5. In what ways do I think of others first rather than of myself?

6. Do I base most of my judgments on what others think or what others might say, or can I differ from others in my thinking?

Skill: I understand the strengths and weaknesses in my family of origin and how those may affect me in my relationships.

1. What strengths do I see in my family of origin, aspects of my family of which I am especially proud?
2. What weaknesses do I see in my family of origin? If I could change one aspect of my family, what would it be?
3. One event or situation that affected my whole family system was _____ . The way it affected me in particular was _____ .
4. How am I different from my family of origin?
5. One way that my family of origin affects the way I relate to others is _____ .

Skill: I communicate and listen effectively, and I am aware of the dynamics of the communication process.

1. Can I clearly say what I'm feeling or what I need, or do others have a hard time reading me?
2. Do others see me as a good listener? Do I find it hard to pay attention to what someone is saying without comparing his or her situation to my own?

SKILLS REVIEW AND BLESSING PRAYER

3. Do I let those close to me know when something bothers me — even something little — or do I keep it inside? If I do bring it up, do I bring it up promptly, or do I put it off?

4. Are my nonverbal signals, like eye contact, facial expressions, and posture, usually consistent with what I'm saying?

5. Do I find it difficult to talk with others, or do I talk too much? If so, am I aware of these problems and trying to address them?

Skill: I am aware of gender and role issues in contemporary culture and how they can affect a marriage, and I am able to communicate about them.

1. What does being feminine or masculine mean to me?

2. What limits do I see to my own gender, masculine or feminine?

3. How do I react to generalizations about men or women?

4. What do I think it would be like to be the opposite gender?

5. What examples are there of automatic roles based on gender in my family of origin, for example, doing the dishes, cooking, paying bills, doing yard work, and washing the car?

SKILLS REVIEW AND BLESSING PRAYER

6. What do I expect of someone of the opposite gender when it comes to doing the dishes, cooking, paying bills, doing yard work, and washing the car?

Skill: I am aware of and comfortable with my own sexuality, that of the opposite sex, and sexuality in general.

1. Am I able to talk about sexuality without embarrassment, using proper terminology?

2. Can I reasonably discuss matters related to sexuality — such as masturbation, homosexuality, and premarital sex — or do I get uncomfortable or adamant?

3. Am I comfortable with my own sexuality and my sexual thoughts and fantasies?

4. Am I comfortable with my own body and see it as attractive, although perhaps not perfect by some standards?

5. Do I see sexuality as an area in which I need to compete with others in order to be considered attractive?

6. Am I comfortable with those of the opposite sex as friends and coworkers?

7. How well balanced is my life — physically, mentally, and emotionally?

Skill: I am aware of my attitudes toward and expectations about money and work and am able to talk about them.

1. What were the attitudes toward money and work in my family of origin? How have I been affected by those attitudes?

2. Complete the following statement at least three different ways: For me, money is _____ .

3. Do I see myself as a spender or a saver? Why?

4. What is something that I see as a need, while others may see it as a want? Why the difference?

5. What is my greatest strength in money management? What is my greatest weakness?

6. For me, the best part of my work is _____ .

7. For me, the worst part of my work is _____ .

8. What one aspect of my work would I change?

Skill: I am able to articulate my own beliefs and spirituality and to respect the spirituality of others.

1. Complete the following statement five different ways: About myself, I believe that _____ .

2. Complete the following statement five different ways: About other people, I believe that _____ .

3. Complete the following statement five different ways: About God, I believe that _____ .

SKILLS REVIEW AND BLESSING PRAYER

4. Complete the following statement five different ways: It has always been important to me that _____ .

5. Complete the following statement five different ways: Ten years from now I would like to _____ .

6. For me, church is _____ .

7. I nourish my own spirituality by _____ .

8. I have been able to share my beliefs and spirituality with _____ .

Skill: I am open to having children and to the ways that being a parent may stretch me to grow.

1. I'm glad my parents _____ .

2. I wish my parents had _____ .

3. I am least comfortable around children when _____ .

4. I am most comfortable around children when _____ .

5. When I picture myself as a parent I _____ .

6. I think children [could] help me _____ .

Skill: I appreciate marriage as a process and as a commitment to change and growth.

1. What commitment have I honored — to a person or an organization or a daily routine of exercise or prayer? Has fidelity to that commitment been freeing for me? If so, how?

2. How is my faithfulness to others linked with being faithful to myself?
3. What are examples of my own generosity?
4. What are examples of my own selfishness?
5. How well do I handle transition and growth in my life and relationships?
6. In what relationship(s) in my life have I experienced the cycle of falling in love, settling down, bottoming out, and beginning again?
7. I/we will revisit this skills review on _____ .

My Blessing Prayer for You

I ask God to be with you in a special way as you consider the sacred vocation of marriage:

May you know well the treasure that you are and be able to spend the time you need in solitude.

May you understand more fully with each passing year what real love and intimacy are, and not be afraid to share yourself deeply.

May you continue to grow in maturity, clarity of values, responsibility, and commitment.

May you grow in your understanding of your family of origin and the ways it has helped you become who you are.

May you grow in your ability to communicate, to listen, to be open and clear, so that you are able to talk about anything.

May you continue to clarify the ways in which gender expectations and messages can affect you and your relationships.

May you see the goodness of your sexuality, and may all your lovemaking be a delightful celebration of life.

May money and work be helpful tools for you, serving you and others rather than being burdens.

May you know the depth of your own spirituality and respect that of others, seeing the love of spouses as a visible sign of a God who is love.

May you accept children lovingly, and may they teach you as much as you teach them about the holiness of each moment.

May you value the gift of change as you flourish through many years of sharing the love God has given you.

Amen.

SKILLS REVIEW AND BLESSING PRAYER

Appendix: Tools for Marriage Preparation and Enrichment

If I have met someone who seems to be the right person and both of us seem to be ready for marriage in terms of the skills discussed in this book, then what helps are available to us to prepare well for our life together? If, on the other hand, we already have begun our lives together and realize that we need further skills and ideas or help on a particular issue, where do we turn? Listed below are resources available for marriage preparation, followed by tools for marriage enrichment.

There are several kinds of resources available for couples, many of which come from the Catholic Church, which has accomplished a great deal in the area of marriage preparation in the past twenty-five years. This is largely due to the Catholic experience of dealing with the pain of marital breakup for those seeking church annulments through diocesan marriage tribunals. Most of these couples had not been adequately prepared for what they were committing themselves to in the first place.

Marriage Preparation Programs

Two main kinds of marriage preparation resources are *programs* of various formats and *issue inventories*. Programs for marriage preparation may range from weekends to a single-day format or a series of several evenings or afternoons; they may be located in the parish or be diocesan or regional in origin. These programs may include the following:

- *Engaged Encounter,* a weekend retreat, is usually led by a priest and two married couples. The retreat offers engaged couples an intensive time together away from other distractions and pressures. The couples concentrate on sharing their issues and concerns after a talk is presented to them on a given topic. Some dioceses also have their own weekend format for marriage preparation. Although this format can be more expensive than some of the other options, it is an excellent opportunity for couples to leave other concerns behind and focus on their relationship, if their schedules can allow a weekend away. For a local number, call (800) 811-3661.

- *Evenings for the Engaged or Pre-Cana Conferences* are a series of evenings or afternoons in a parish or regional setting that allows a single presenter or several speakers to offer material on key topics, such as communication, finances, sexuality, and spirituality, and to encourage couple discussion about the issues presented. These sessions are usually not as intense as the weekend format but are helpful for couples who are unable to attend a weekend. This format allows couples to interact with other couples who are also beginning their marriages.

- *Sponsor Couple* programs pair one or more engaged couples with a married couple from their parish who hosts them in their home for a series of sessions about topics similar to those mentioned above. This gives the married folks the opportunity to mentor the couple or couples in light of their experience of marriage in the real world. It also provides the possibility for follow-up contact, assuming the newlyweds stay in the area. Interestingly, this mentoring is already built into the Hispanic tradition of *padrinos,* couples designated to help support the new couple. This program may be more flexible in terms of time compared with other programs.

Catholic parishes or diocesan family life offices should have information about the local availability of these programs. Other churches and local social service agencies may offer programs as well. An increasing number of communities have a community marriage policy among the local churches, agreeing that none will host weddings without a minimal amount of marriage preparation. Check with your Council of Churches or ecumenical organization to find out about local resources.

Marriage Preparation Inventories

There are several inventories available that give both the couple and a priest or other professional working with the couple an overview of the couple's strengths and weaknesses, including information about issues that may need more discussion.

To use one of the relationship inventories as a pass/fail determinant of whether the couple is ready to get married would be a misuse of the tool; rather, each is designed as a springboard for discussion of issues, especially those that may have been overlooked or may be especially problematic for a couple. These tools include the following:

- *FOCCUS* (Facilitating Open Couple Communication Understanding and Study) was developed by the Archdiocese of Omaha, Nebraska, and has been recently revised. In addition to the usual categories "Lifestyle Expectations," "Friends and Interests," "Personality Match," "Personal Issues," "Communication," "Problem Solving," "Religion and Values," "Parenting," "Extended

Family," "Sexuality," and "Financial and Readiness Issues," this tool also includes an explicit focus on the sacrament of marriage. Other important issues considered in the tool are family of origin and dual careers. It also includes sections for couples with special issues, such as interfaith marriages or second marriages or cohabitation. The printout that is generated from the couple's answers gives both the couple and the counselor working with them valuable information to consider as they look at the relationship. For more information, contact FOCCUS, Family Life Office, 3214 N. 60th, Omaha, NE 68104, (402) 551-9003. (FOCCUS is also available in Spanish, braille, and audiotape versions.)

- *The Premarital Inventory,* or PMI, one of the earliest such resources, has now been revised as the PMI Profile, which explores topics similar to those that are explored in FOCCUS. For more information, contact PMI Profile, Intercommunications Publishing, Inc., 1 Valentine Lane, Chapel Hill, NC 27514.

- *PREPARE* (PREmarital Personal And Relationship Evaluation) gives a profile of some of the issues on which the partners may agree and disagree. In addition to topics addressed by FOCCUS and the PMI, this tool also considers the topics "Idealistic Distortion," "Leisure Activities," "Realistic Expectations," and "Realistic

Orientation." Training is encouraged for those who facilitate PREPARE. More information is available from PREPARE-ENRICH, Inc., P.O. Box 190, Minneapolis, MN 55440-0190.

These programs and inventories are no substitute for one-on-one contact with the priest or deacon presiding at the wedding and perhaps a counselor trained in marriage preparation.

A recent follow-up study of marriage preparation in the Catholic Church (see Center for Marriage and Family below) found that most couples consider their marriage preparation process to be of significant value, especially when presented by a team over several sessions and dealing with the five Cs: communication, commitment, conflict resolution, children, and church. Another C, dual careers, which is increasingly common, evidently needs more emphasis. Interfaith couples also need more specific attention to their unique needs.

Studies, of course, cannot statistically assure us that couples with strong, formal marriage preparation are less prone to divorce. The informal experience of couples, however, seems to bear out the importance of time spent before the wedding to help assure the success of the marriage. The more prepared we are as a couple for the many demands and adjustments that lie ahead, the better. As the motto for Engaged Encounter puts it, "A wedding is a day; a marriage is a lifetime."

Other Resources for Engaged Couples

Brennan, Patrick, ed. *Marriage Is More Than You and Me: Reflections for Engaged Couples Entering Catholic Matrimony.* Chicago: ACTA Publications, 1992. This book explores fourteen key concerns of couples preparing for marriage.

Cavanagh, Michael E. *Before the Wedding: Look Before You Leap.* Louisville: Westminster/John Knox, 1994. Reflections for engaged couples or those considering marriage, this book includes sections on cautions and problems.

Center for Marriage and Family, Creighton University. *Marriage Preparation in the Catholic Church: Getting It Right.* Omaha: Creighton University, November 1995. A report on a follow-up study of couples using the FOCCUS inventory, this resource is appropriate for parish ministers.

Champlin, Joseph M. *Together for Life.* Notre Dame, Ind.: Ave Maria Press, 1970. This popular resource for planning the wedding ceremony comes in two versions — with a Mass or without. It is also available in Spanish from Liguori Publications.

Finley, Mitch. *Married Love: A Special Way of Being Alive.* Chicago: ACTA Publications, 1990. Finley offers helpful perspectives on several issues for engaged couples.

Healey, James. *Living Together and the Christian Commitment: A Reflection for Couples Who Are Living*

Together. Allen, Tex.: Tabor, 1993. Healey's book provides brief, nonjudgmental material for couples already living together. A leader's guide is also available.

Heaney-Hunter, Joann, and Louis Primavera. *Unitas: Preparing for Sacramental Marriage.* New York: Crossroad, 1998. Based on the Rite of Christian Initiation for Adults, this is a program of seven sessions — complete with videotapes — for engaged couples.

Larsen, Earnie. *Getting It Right: A Self-Directed Program for Engaged Couples.* Chicago: ACTA Publications, 1996. These audiotapes offer an alternative or supplemental marriage preparation.

Midgley, John, and Susan Midgley. *A Decision to Love: A Marriage Preparation Program.* Mystic, Conn.: Twenty-Third Publications, 1992. This flexible resource includes a couple's book with excellent his-and-her pages and several suggested formats as well as a leader's guide.

Perspectives on Marriage. Chicago: ACTA Publications, 1998. Recently revised, this resource includes a variety of exercise sheets and a leader's guide for help in planning programs and presentations.

Thomas, John L. *Beginning Your Marriage.* Revised by David M. Thomas. 8th ed. Chicago: ACTA Publications, 1994. A classic resource for engaged couples, Thomas's book is filled with information. (For more suggestions for engaged couples, see the appendix, "Tools for Marriage Preparation and Enrichment," on page 194.)

United States Catholic Conference. *Faithful to Each Other Forever: A Catholic Handbook of Pastoral Help for Marriage Preparation.* Washington, D.C.: United States Catholic Conference, 1989. This handbook presents summary information for parish staffs.

Marriage Enrichment Resources

When married people come face-to-face with issues that make loving each other a harder job than when their relationship was new, where do they turn? Many social-service agencies and local churches offer helpful programs on marital communication and enrichment. Marriage counseling is also an option for couples who are struggling with severe relationship issues; it is especially valuable as a preventive measure, giving a couple the opportunity to identify and work on problem areas before they reach overwhelming proportions. Three other resources available throughout the country are worth mentioning:

- *PREP* (Prevention and Relationship Enhancement Program), also called Fighting for Your Marriage, is an excellent skills-based program dealing with communication and conflict resolution. Based on solid long-term research — and now affirmed by follow-up research —

this program gives couples tools that will help them reach consensus in those areas where they disagree. Couples have the opportunity to exercise these tools in the course of the sessions. For more information and locations where it may be offered, call (303) 756-9931. This program is also available on audiotape and video-tape as well as in book form. (See the entry for Scott Stanley in "Suggested Reading," page 208.) For book or tape orders, call (800) 366-0166.

- *Marriage Encounter* is a weekend-format experience that helps people enhance their communication as a couple and to rekindle the love that brought them together in the first place. It encourages and teaches a dialogue process that allows couples to continue growing closer through the years. For more information, call (800) 828-3351 for National Marriage Encounter or (800) 795-LOVE ([800] 795-5683) for Worldwide Marriage Encounter. (Both weekends are similar.)

- *REFOCCUS* (Relationship Enrichment Facilitating Open Couple Communication, Understanding and Study) is an instrument for marriage enrichment published by the authors of the FOCCUS program for engaged couples. This program may be used by individual couples or in a group setting for marriage enrichment. It consists of five sections, "Marriage as a Process," "Intimacy," "Compatibility," "Communication," and "Commitment." For each part, the spouses mark their answers to fifteen to twenty statements and then discuss their answers. This resource allows flexibility and clarity for the couple using it. For more information, call (402) 551-9003.

- *RETROUVAILLE* ("Rediscovery") is a weekend program designed for couples in hurting marriages who may be separating, separated, or even divorced and are thinking about reconciliation. While Catholic in origin, the weekend is open to all faiths and is presented by a priest and couples who have themselves been through a rebuilding of their relationship. For more information, call (800) 470-2230.

What about Marriage Counseling?

Should a husband and wife consult a counselor about issues that seem too big for them to handle well alone, or is marriage counseling just for those on the edge of a divorce? If they do decide to see a marriage counselor, how do they find a competent one?

A marriage counselor can be a helpful resource to a couple and should ideally be consulted long before the situation becomes unmanageable. A good counselor gives both spouses a chance to talk out their concerns with an impartial third party who can call their attention to issues they may be overlooking. Ideally, husband and wife see the marriage counselor together, but if one spouse refuses to go, the other can benefit by going alone to sort out the issues involved.

In an article titled "How Our Marriage Was Saved" (*Parents Magazine*, August 1993), author Ann Campbell quotes marriage and family counselor Dr. Evelyn Bassoff, who offers the following checklist of concerns that may be reasons for consulting a professional counselor:

- We fight a lot.
- We have trouble communicating; my spouse just doesn't understand.
- We can't agree on how to raise our child.
- We need help making a major decision (e.g., whether to have another baby, move, or make a career change).
- We need help dealing with other family members (e.g., in-laws, stepchildren).
- We need help dealing with a major crisis (such as illness in the family, birth of a child with special needs, financial loss).
- We are having conflicts in our sex life.
- We are drifting apart.
- I feel suffocated in our marriage.
- I feel unloved or taken for granted by my spouse.

- I'm afraid of my spouse.
- I don't trust my spouse.
- I'm unhappy being married, but I don't know why.

Finding the right counselor can be challenging, however. Knowledgeable friends or a reputable local social-service agency can be sources for good referrals. Another source is the American Association of Marriage and Family Therapists (AAMFT), which accredits professionals in this field. The association can be reached at 1717 K Street NW, Suite 407, Washington, DC 20006. An initial session should give you a sense of whether or not you will be able to work with a particular counselor.

Asking for Help Is OK

Whether for marriage preparation or marriage enrichment, time spent on relationship issues is definitely a good investment, giving a couple the chance to deal with issues before they grow to the point where they can overwhelm the relationship. Although there is still some strong cultural resistance to asking for help or seeking counseling, asking for help is, in fact, the healthy move for a husband and wife when the issues are more than they can handle by themselves.

Suggested Reading

Finley, Mitch, and Kathy Finley. *Building Christian Families.* Allen, Tex.: Thomas More, 1996. Originally published in 1984, this book explores some of the main aspects of families as the basic form of church.

Gottman, John. *Why Marriages Succeed or Fail . . . and How You Can Make Yours Last.* New York: Simon and Schuster, 1994. Based on solid research, Gottman's book provides useful information and exercises for couples to strengthen their communication.

Peck, M. Scott. *The Road Less Traveled: A New Psychology of Love, Traditional Values, and Spiritual Growth.* New York: Simon and Schuster, 1978. This best-seller offers many insights into personal growth that are helpful to both couples and individuals.

Penner, Clifford L., and Joyce J. Penner. *Getting Your Sex Life Off to a Great Start: A Guide for Engaged and Newlywed Couples.* Dallas: Word Publishing, 1994. This book is filled with helpful information and wisdom. While the chapter on family planning is respectful of official church teachings on the topic, it does not conform to it.

Pipher, Mary. *The Shelter of Each Other: Rebuilding Our Families.* New York: Ballantine, 1996. Pipher's book, especially the first chapter, makes helpful observations about the context in which family life takes place today.

Powell, John. *Why Am I Afraid to Tell You Who I Am? Insights into Personal Growth.* Allen, Tex.: Tabor, 1995; *Why Am I Afraid to Love? Overcoming Rejection and Indifference.* Allen, Tex.: Tabor, 1990. Powell offers two clearly written classics on relationships and intimacy.

Stanley, Scott, et al. *A Lasting Promise: A Christian Guide to Fighting for Your Marriage.* San Francisco: Jossey-Bass, 1998. Based on the excellent and well-researched PREP (Prevention and Relationship Enhancement Program), this book teaches important skills in a Christian context. *Fighting for Your Marriage: Positive Steps for Preventing Divorce and Preserving a Lasting Love* by Howard Markman, et al. (San Francisco: Jossey-Bass, 1994) also presents these skills.

Tannen, Deborah. *You Just Don't Understand: Women and Men in Conversation.* New York: Ballantine, 1990.

SUGGESTED READING

This book is a helpful resource on gender issues in communication.

United States Catholic Conference. *Follow the Way of Love: A Pastoral Message of the U.S. Catholic Bishops to Families.* Washington, D.C.: United States Catholic Conference, 1994. This is a short, easy-to-read booklet on the everyday holiness of family life.

SUGGESTED READING

Bibliography

Anzia, Joan, and Mary Durkin. *Marital Intimacy: A Catholic Perspective.* Chicago: Loyola Press, 1980.

Berends, Polly Berrien. *Gently Lead: How to Teach Your Children about God While Finding Out for Yourself.* Rev. ed. New York: Crossroad, 1998.

Briggs, Dorothy Corkille. *Your Child's Self-Esteem: The Key to His Life.* Garden City, N.Y.: Doubleday, 1975.

Catechism of the Catholic Church. Washington, D.C.: United States Catholic Conference, 1994.

Crosby, James. *Illusion and Disillusion.* Belmont, Calif.: Wadsworth Publishing, 1976.

Fromm, Erich. *The Art of Loving.* New York: Bantam, 1956.

Healy, James. *Living Together and the Christian Commitment.* Allen, Tex.: Tabor, 1993.

Ho, Man Keung. *Building a Successful Intermarriage between Religions, Social Classes, Ethnic Groups, or Races.* St. Meinrad, Ind.: Abbey Press, 1984.

Kavanaugh, John, S.J. *Following Christ in a Consumer Society: The Spirituality of Cultural Resistance.* Rev. ed. Maryknoll, N.Y.: Orbis, 1991.

Kennedy, Eugene. *The Trouble Book.* New York: Simon and Schuster, 1977.

LeMaire, H. Paul. *Marrying Takes a Lifetime.* Mystic, Conn.: Twenty-Third Publications, 1981.

McManus, Michael J. *Marriage Savers: Helping Your Friends and Family Stay Married.* Grand Rapids, Mich.: Zondervan, 1993.

Montagu, Ashley. *Touching: The Human Significance of the Skin.* New York: Harper and Row, 1971.

Old Farmer's Almanac. "How to Find Your Perfect Mate." Dublin, N.H.: Yankee Publishing, 1986.

Peck, M. Scott. *The Road Less Traveled: A New Psychology of Love, Traditional Values, and Spiritual Growth.* New York: Simon and Schuster, 1978.

Pipher, Mary. *The Shelter of Each Other: Rebuilding Our Families.* New York: Ballantine, 1996.

Powell, John. *Why Am I Afraid to Tell You Who I Am? Insights into Personal Growth.* Allen, Tex.: Tabor, 1995.

Roberts, William. *Marriage: Sacrament of Hope and Challenge.* Cincinnati: St. Anthony Messenger Press, 1988.

Russell, Mary Doria. *The Sparrow.* New York: Ballantine, 1996.

Saint-Exupèry, Antoine de. *The Little Prince.* New York: Harcourt, Brace, 1943.

Schlessinger, Laura. *Ten Stupid Things Women Do to Mess Up Their Lives.* New York: Villard, 1995.

Shelton, Robert. *Loving Relationships: Self, Others, and God.* Elgin, Ill.: Brethren Press, 1987.

Tannen, Deborah. *Talking from 9 to 5.* New York: William Morrow, 1994.

———. *You Just Don't Understand: Women and Men in Conversation.* New York: Ballantine, 1990.

Thomas, John L. *Beginning Your Marriage.* 7th ed. Chicago: ACTA Publications, 1987.

Whitehead, Evelyn Eaton, and James D. Whitehead. *Marrying Well: Possibilities in Christian Marriage Today.* Garden City, N.Y.: Doubleday, 1981.